First Language Lessons

for the Well-Trained Mind

Level 2

by Jessie Wise

Peace Hill Press
www.peacehillpress.com

Publisher's Cataloging-In-Publication Data

(Prepared by The Donohue Group, Inc.)

Wise, Jessie.
   First language lessons for the well-trained mind. Level 2 / by Jessie Wise.

      p. : ill. ; cm.

   Includes index.
   ISBN: 978-1-933339-45-0

1. English language--Grammar--Study and teaching (Primary) 2. English language--Composition and exercises--Study and teaching (Primary) 3. Language arts (Primary) I. Title.

LB1528 .W574 2010
372.61

For children everywhere—
and for my grandchildren especially

TABLE OF CONTENTS

How to Use This Book xii

Lesson 1 1
Nouns

Lesson 2 3
Poem memorization: "The Goops"
Copywork: "The Goops"

Lesson 3 5
Pronouns
Copywork: "Emily sang"
Poem review: "The Goops" (Lesson 2)

Lesson 4 7
Verbs (action verbs)
Capitalizing "I"
Copywork: "The baby and I"
Poem review: "The Goops" (Lesson 2)

Lesson 5 9
Introducing state of being verbs
Copywork: State of being verbs
Poem review: "The Goops" (Lesson 2)

Lesson 6 11
State of being verbs

Lesson 7 13
Introducing linking verbs
Poem review: "The Goops" (Lesson 2)

Lesson 8 16
Linking verbs

Lesson 9 17
Story narration: "The Camel's Nose"

Lesson 10 20
Linking verbs

Lesson 11 22
Beginning poem booklet
Copywork: "The Year"
Poem review: "The Goops" (Lesson 2)

Lesson 12 24
Four types of sentences
Seasons
Copywork: "January"

Lesson 13 26
Commas (dates and addresses)
Copywork: "February"

Lesson 14 28
Commas in a series
Copywork: "Snuggles, wiggles, grins, and giggles"
Poem review: "The Goops" (Lesson 2)

Lesson 15 30
Introducing helping verbs
Copywork: "March"

Lesson 16 34
Noun review
Verb review
Copywork: "April"

Lesson 17 37
Capitalization (proper names, initials, titles of respect, addresses, poems)

Lesson 18 40
   Introducing picture narration: "Dick and
   Lawless in Holyrood Forest" by N. C.
   Wyeth

Lesson 19 42
   Contractions
   Copywork: Contractions

Lesson 20 44
   Contractions
   Copywork: Contractions

Lesson 21 46
   Contractions using "not"
   Copywork: "May"

Lesson 22 49
   Introducing dictation: "March"

Lesson 23 51
   Introducing adjectives
   Copywork: "June"

Lesson 24 53
   Adjectives
   Copywork: "July"

Lesson 25 55
   Nouns
   Pronouns
   Verbs
   Adjectives
   Copywork: "August"

Lesson 26 58
   Helping verbs
   Dictation exercise: "God has made them so"
   Copywork: "September"

Lesson 27 61
   Story narration: "The Quarrel"

Lesson 28 63
   Contractions
   Copywork: "October"
   Poem review: "The Goops" (Lesson 2)

Lesson 29 65
   Four kinds of verbs review
   Copywork: "November"

Lesson 30 67
   Adjectives
   Copywork: "December"

Lesson 31 68
   Poem memorization: "The Year"

Lesson 32 70
   Introducing interjections
   Four types of sentences
   Copywork: "Ouch!"
   Poem review: "The Year" (Lesson 31)

Lesson 33 73
   Adjectives
   Commas in a series
   Dictation exercise: "The brown bird"
   Poem review: "The Year" (Lesson 31)

Lesson 34 75
   Parts of Speech
   Introducing conjunctions
   Dictation exercise: "I was tired"
   Poem review: "The Year" (Lesson 31)

Lesson 35 78
Interjections
Conjunctions
Dictation exercise: "The zoo"
Poem review: "The Goops" (Lesson 2)

Lesson 36 81
Introducing letter-writing: Writing a thank-you note
Poem review: "The Year" (Lesson 31)

Lesson 37 83
Addressing an envelope

Lesson 38 84
Introducing direct quotations
Quotation marks
Copywork: "The Little Bird"

Lesson 39 86
Poem memorization: "The Little Bird"

Lesson 40 87
Story narration: "The Little Red Hen"
Copywork: "The Little Red Hen"
Poem review: "The Little Bird" (Lesson 39)

Lesson 41 91
Introducing indirect quotations
Copywork: "Not I"
Poem review: "The Little Bird" (Lesson 39)

Lesson 42 93
Titles of respect
Adjectives
Quotation marks
Dictation exercise: "Who will help me?"

Lesson 43 96
Four types of sentences
Dictation exercise: "The dump truck"
Poem review: "The Little Bird" (Lesson 39)

Lesson 44 101
Story narration: "The Three Billy Goats Gruff"
Poem review: "The Year" (Lesson 31)

Lesson 45 104
Quotations
Four types of sentences
Parts of speech
Dictation exercise: "I'm coming to eat you up!"

Lesson 46 106
Picture narration: "At this the whole pack rose up into the air..." by Arthur Rackham

Lesson 47 108
Introducing adverbs
Dictation exercise: "I ate my supper"
Poem review: "The Year" (Lesson 31)

Lesson 48 110
Adverbs
Dictation exercise: "Whole Duty of Children"
Poem review: "The Little Bird" (Lesson 39)

Lesson 49 112
Addresses
Copywork: Addressing postcards

Lesson 50 114
Writing postcards
Nouns
Adjectives
Copywork: "Writing Postcards"
Poem review: "The Goops" (Lesson 2)

Lesson 51 116
  Dates
  Months of the year
  Seasons
  Days of the week
  Copywork: Remembering the days of the week

Lesson 52 119
  Four kinds of verbs
  Dictation exercise: "Dinosaurs"

Lesson 53 122
  Adverbs
  Adjectives
  Poem review: "The Year" (Lesson 31)

Lesson 54 124
  Story narration: "The Storm"

Lesson 55 126
  Adjectives
  Adverbs

Lesson 56 129
  Introducing articles
  Dictation exercise: "What we did"

Lesson 57 132
  Articles
  Capitalization review

Lesson 58 135
  Introducing prepositions
  Dictation exercise: "Over my head"
  Poem review: "The Little Bird" (Lesson 39)

Lesson 59 138
  Prepositions
  Poem review: "The Year" (Lesson 31)

Lesson 60 140
  Picture narration: "The Great Wave off Kanagawa" by Katsushika Hokusai

Lesson 61 142
  Prepositions
  Dictation exercise: "Bed in Summer"

Lesson 62 145
  Prepositions
  Dictation exercise: "Beneath the pyramids"

Lesson 63 147
  Prepositions
  Dictation exercise: "Beneath the castle wall"
  Poem review: "The Goops" (Lesson 2)

Lesson 64 150
  Articles
  Commas in a series
  Conjunctions
  Prepositions
  Dictation exercise: "During my lesson"

Lesson 65 153
  Prepositions
  Adverbs

Lesson 66 155
  Prepositions
  Verbs

Lesson 67 158
  Prepositions
  Dictation exercise: "King of the stuffed animals"
  Poem review: "The Little Bird" (Lesson 39)

Lesson 68 160
Prepositions
Dictation exercise: "Through the rain"

Lesson 69 163
Cumulative poem review

Lesson 70 164
Letter writing: Writing a friendly letter
Prepositions
Copywork: Writing a letter

Lesson 71 166
Addressing an envelope

Lesson 72 168
Prepositions

Lesson 73 172
Story narration: "The Three Bears"

Lesson 74 176
Introducing synonyms
Dictation exercise: "Roller coasters"

Lesson 75 179
Introducing antonyms
Dictation exercise: "Brush your teeth"

Lesson 76 182
Picture narration: "Snowy Owls" by John
James Audubon

Lesson 77 185
Four types of sentences
Poem review: "The Year" (Lesson 31)

Lesson 78 186
Verbs
Dictation exercise: "The platypus"

Lesson 79 189
Adverbs
Adjectives

Lesson 80 192
Interjections
Prepositions
Dictation exercise: "Ow! Yuck! Oh!"
Poem review: "The Goops" (Lesson 2)

Lesson 81 195
Direct and indirect quotations
Dictation exercise: "Who's that trip-
trapping?"

Lesson 82 198
Nouns
Pronouns
Dictation exercise: "The mother cat"
Poem review: "The Little Bird" (Lesson 39)

Lesson 83 201
Contractions
Copywork: Contractions

Lesson 84 204
Picture narration: "Snap the Whip" by
Winslow Homer

Lesson 85 207
Poem memorization: "All Things Bright and
Beautiful"

Lesson 86 208
Cumulative review

Lesson 87 211
Cumulative review

Lesson 88 213
    Cumulative review

Lesson 89 215
    Prepositions
    Poem review: "All Things Bright and
      Beautiful" (Lesson 85)

Lesson 90 217
    Synonyms
    Antonyms
    Dictation exercise: "The troll"
    Poem review: "All Things Bright and
      Beautiful" (Lesson 85)

Lesson 91 220
    Parts of speech review
    Poem review: "All Things Bright and
      Beautiful" (Lesson 85)

Lesson 92 222
    Picture narration: "One of the Family" by
      Frederick George Cotman

Lesson 93 224
    Review of memorized lists

Lesson 94 225
    Homophones
    Poem review: "All Things Bright and
      Beautiful" (Lesson 85)

Lesson 95 227
    Cumulative poem review

Lesson 96 228
    Dictation exercise: Review session 1

Lesson 97 229
    Dictation exercise: Review session 2

Lesson 98 230
    Dictation exercise: Review session 3

Lesson 99 231
    Story narration: "The Donkey and the Salt"

Lesson 100 233
    Parts of speech hunt

Glossary of Term and Definitions 235

Poems 238

How to Use This Book

I believe we underestimate what young children are capable of learning. Our ideas are influenced by the school model, which aims most of its instruction at what it considers the largest population—the "average child." But when we teach to the average, we train our children to be…average! Instead, we can grow children who exceed the average by exposing them to above-average content—as long as that content is taught patiently, frequently, and consistently, and is reviewed often.

General Thoughts on Teaching Language

Learning rules without practical application is a sterile activity. Absorbing grammar incidentally without the guidance of rules is inefficient. By combining simple rules with continued "real life" use of those rules in language, the teacher lays the foundation for a child's application of appropriate rules to his own work in the future.

Children are natural imitators. This book provides you with examples of correctly spoken and written English in order to train the child's ear and hand. Then his original ideas can have form and beauty when they are expressed.

Every time a child speaks or writes correctly, that pattern is imprinted on his mind; the same is true for patterns that are incorrectly practiced. It is better to do less work, and do it correctly, than to practice errors. Then the child doesn't have to spend time unlearning and relearning.

So don't hurry through these lessons just to finish. Take the time to have the child answer in complete sentences. Take the time to frequently repeat rules until the child knows them. Take the time to have the child write correctly. Take the time to allow the child to make corrections immediately. If you require him to correct his mistakes, you will not damage his self-esteem. Compliment the correction and you will build his confidence.

Do not wait until a child is reading to expose him to good literature. Likewise, do not wait until a child is writing to expose him to proper use of our language. This is why I encourage the use of oral exercises while the child is young. Speech patterns are developed early. The longer a child uses incorrect language, the harder it will be to teach him correct speech and writing.

This early exposure is the purpose of my introducing young children to what some may consider advanced material. But this early introduction is not intended to result in mastery; mastery comes later.

I suggest you file the child's work in a notebook. This will serve as a way to organize all of his language work—narrations that you write for him, his copy work and dictations, his exercises, and copies of the letters he writes to real people.

The Method of This Book

First Language Lessons for the Well-Trained Mind combines the best of traditional content with examples and illustrations meaningful to present-day children. The scripted lessons focus on training the child in the proper use of standard English. They are not intended to be read by the child—instead, they aim to give you some idea of how to teach these skills. Appropriate answers that the child should give to your questions are suggested, but the child should certainly not be required to give those answers word for word! Do remember, though, to require all answers in complete sentences. If the child answers with a single word or phrase, reword the answer as a complete sentence, repeat it to the child, and ask him to repeat it back to you. This will begin to train his ear to recognize complete sentences.

This book covers grammar skills for grade 2. You will also need to provide a phonics/spelling program, formal penmanship instruction, and a writing program. *The Ordinary Parent's Guide to Teaching Reading* (phonics) and *Writing With Ease* (writing), both published by Peace Hill Press, are designed to be completely compatible with *First Language Lessons*.

An elementary writing curriculum is recommended because *First Language Lessons* covers grammar but does not cover beginning composition. The young writer should be encouraged to write across the curriculum, rather than doing isolated writing exercises related only to his grammar lessons. *Writing With Ease* by Susan Wise Bauer, also published by Peace Hill Press, is a step-by-step guide to developing elementary writing skills. The lessons are coordinated with *First Language Lessons* so that grammar concepts taught here are then reinforced by the *Writing With Ease* assignments.

Goals for Grade 2
1. To train the child's ear by allowing him to listen to correctly spoken language.
2. To train the child's speech by practicing correctly spoken grammar with him.
3. To train the child's attention by reading aloud to him and having him narrate back to you the content or story line, using proper grammar.
4. To teach beginning skills in correct grammar, capitalization, and punctuation.

Remember: exposure, not mastery, is the goal at this level!

The Tools Used in This Book: The "Four Strand" Approach
This book teaches rules, usage, and beginning writing skills by using four different tools.

Strand 1: Memory work
The child is assigned simple memory work—short poems and brief rules and definitions to learn by heart. The poems instill the beauty and rhythm of correct language in the child's mind. The rules and definitions may not be completely understood when they are first committed to memory, but they will be a resource for the child as he[1] continues to exercise his growing language skills.

Strand 2: Copying and dictation
The student is asked both to copy sentences and to take sentences from dictation. These exercises do not replace a writing program; they specifically target particular grammar skills.

Strand 3: Narration
While the student is studying the basic principles of grammar, he is also learning how to produce original content orally. This will allow him to practice correct grammar at a time when he is still too young for extensive written work.

Two types of narration are used; both are intended to train the child in attention, observation, and expression, so that as he matures he will be able to share his own thoughts with eloquence.

---

1   **A note on inclusive pronouns:** I studied advanced traditional grammar in the 1950s as part of my training in teacher certification. I learned that the pronouns "he" and "him" were generic pronouns, used to refer to both men and women. Although I understand why some users would prefer to see an alternate use of "he" and "she," I find this style of writing awkward; my early training shapes my usage! So I have used "he" and "him" to refer to the child throughout. If you prefer, simply change these pronouns to "she" and "her."

a. Picture narration. Some of the lessons ask the student to look at and describe a picture. This allows him to practice observation skills as well as proper language use—always encourage the child to describe the picture in complete sentences!

b. Story narration. In other lessons, you will read a short story to the child and then ask him to tell it back to you in his own words. This type of narration helps the child to listen with attention, to comprehend spoken language, and to grasp the main point of a work.

Strand 4: Grammar

The rules of grammar bring order to the chaos of words in the child's mind. Think of the study of formal grammar as the building of a room. The essentials—nouns and verbs—are the floor, walls, and ceiling. The room is decorated with adjectives and adverbs. The relationships between the different pieces of furniture in the room are demonstrated through prepositions and conjunctions. And sometimes the people in the room show intense emotion—with interjections!

The student is taught the correct definitions of grammatical terms from the very beginning.

I assume that many children will not be ready to do a great deal of pencil-work in second grade. For children who are physically capable of doing more writing, I have provided enrichment activities. But it is not necessary—or expected—that most children will do these enrichment exercises!

Plan on doing 2–3 lessons per week. Also plan on reviewing previous lessons as necessary, since the child may not remember material covered earlier.

Using the Lessons

Instructor: Suggested wording for the instructor is in traditional print.

Student: *Suggested wording for the student is in italics.*

Notes to Instructor *are indented, set in smaller type and in italics.*

Suggested wording that the student is to read or follow is in larger traditional print.

Definitions and terms are in larger bold print.

Note to Instructor: *Assume that lessons 1-100 all require that both the instructor and the student have a pencil and paper. Additional supplies will be listed at the beginning of each lesson. If you wish to gather all your supplies in advance, you will need colored pencils, crayons, markers, construction paper, a folder, a highlighter marker, glue, scissors, two or more business-size envelopes, first-class letter stamps, five or more postcards, first-class postcard stamps, a pack of index cards, and a place setting (fork, knife, spoon, plate, glass, napkin). You will also need a dictionary and a thesaurus. My favorites for this age are* Merriam-Webster's Elementary Dictionary *(2009) and* Roget's Children's Thesaurus *(Scott Foresman-Addison Wesley, 1994).*

This book is designed to follow and reinforce *First Language Lessons, Level 1*. Older students may begin with Level 2, but you may wish to stop and practice memorized lists and definitions for a slightly longer period than is suggested here.

9/12/19

Nouns

Instructor: **A noun is the name of a person, place, thing, or idea.** Repeat that definition with me.

TOGETHER: **A noun is the name of a person, place, thing, or idea.**

Instructor: A **common noun** is the name of any person, place, thing, or idea. A **proper noun** is the special, particular name of a person, place, thing, or idea. Repeat the definition of a proper noun with me.

TOGETHER: A proper noun is the special, particular name of a person, place, thing, or idea.

> **Note to Instructor:** *"Proper noun" and "proper name" both have the same meaning.*

Instructor: Is "boy" a proper or common noun?
Student: *"Boy" is a common noun.*

> **Note to Instructor:** *Remember to encourage the student to answer in complete sentences.*

Instructor: Can you give me a proper noun that names a particular boy?
Student: *[name]*

Instructor: Is "girl" a proper or common noun?
Student: *"Girl" is a common noun.*

Instructor: Can you give me a proper noun that names a particular girl?
Student: *[name]*

Instructor: Can you tell me some common nouns that name places?
Student: *[city, park, store, library, room, yard, etc.]*

Instructor: Now, can you think of a proper name for one of these places?
Student: *[Student names familiar proper name for a place]*

> **Note to Instructor:** *Help the student think of a proper name for a store, restaurant, or other familiar landmark.*

Instructor: There are lots and lots of common things in the world. I will name some of them, and I want you to give me proper names for them. The first is "toy." There are many, many toys. What is the proper name of one of your toys?

Student: *[Gives proper brand name of a toy—Legos, Hot Wheels]*

Instructor: Nouns are names of persons, places, and things. Nouns also name ideas. Remember, an idea is something that you can think about or feel, but not touch or see. "Happiness," "joy," "freedom," "sadness," and "excitement" are all nouns. They are names of ideas. Here are some sentences that use "idea" nouns.

Note to Instructor: *Emphasize the names of ideas in the following sentences. Ask the student to follow along as you read.*

Happiness can be shared.

She was filled with joy when her kitty was rescued.

A caged bird has no freedom.

Excitement filled the room during the birthday party.

Sadness makes me want to cry.

I was filled with fear when I was lost.

Instructor: Can you make up a sentence about an idea?

Note to Instructor: *Help the student say out loud complete sentences that have "idea" nouns in them.*

······················· **LESSON 2** ······················

Poem memorization: "The Goops"
Copywork: "The Goops"

Note to Instructor: *The student will need drawing supplies for the enrichment activity.*

Instructor: For this lesson, I am going to read you a poem about the Goops.

The Goops
By Gelett Burgess

The Goops they lick their fingers,
And the Goops they lick their knives;
They spill their broth on the tablecloth-
Oh, they lead disgusting lives!
The Goops they talk while eating,
And loud and fast they chew,
And that is why I'm glad that I
Am not a Goop - are you?

Instructor: The name of a poem—its title—and the first word in every line of poetry should be capitalized. Let's look at the poem "The Goops" together. How many words does the title have in it?

Student: *The title has two words in it.*

Instructor: Both words are capitalized. "The" is capitalized because it is the first word of the title. "Goops" is capitalized because it is an important word in the title. Now run your finger down the left-hand side of the poem. There is a capital letter at the beginning of each line. The first word of every line of a poem should be capitalized. Now we will work on memorizing this poem. I will read it out loud to you three times.

Notes to Instructor: *Read the poem to the student and discuss it before working on memorization. As a helpful technique to assist in memorization, try the following: On the first day that the poem is assigned, read the poem aloud to the student three times in a row. Repeat this triple reading twice more during the day, if possible. After the first day, read the poem aloud three times in a row once daily. (It may be more convenient to read the poem into a tape recorder three times, and then have the student replay the tape.) On the second day, and every day thereafter, ask the student to try to repeat parts of the poem along with you (or the tape recorder). When he can say the poem along with you, encourage him to repeat it first to a stuffed animal, then to himself in a mirror, and finally to "real people."*

Today, read "The Goops" aloud three times in a row. Repeat twice more during the day. Don't forget to say the title and author as part of each repetition!

Copywork

Choose one of the following copywork assignments, depending on the student's ability. You may want to copy the assignment in the style of print that the student is using in his handwriting lessons.

"The Goops"
  By Gelett Burgess

They spill their broth on the tablecloth.

They spill their broth on the tablecloth.
  Oh, they lead disgusting lives!

Enrichment Activity

The student can illustrate the poem "The Goops."

·   **LESSON 3**   · · · · · · · · · · · · · · · · · · ·

9/16

Pronouns
Copywork: "Emily sang"
Poem review: "The Goops" (Lesson 2)

Note to Instructor: *Read "The Goops" three times. Encourage the student to chime in as he is able.*

Instructor: **A pronoun is a word used in the place of a noun.** Let's say that definition together three times.

TOGETHER (three times): **A pronoun is a word used in the place of a noun.**

Instructor: You use the pronouns "I," "me," "my," "mine" when you talk about yourself. Let's repeat those together three times.

TOGETHER (three times): I, me, my, mine.

Instructor: Can you use the pronoun "mine" in a sentence?
Student: *[gives sentence]*

Note to Instructor: *Prompt student, if necessary, to use the pronoun correctly.*

Instructor: The pronouns "you," "your," "yours" can take the place of the person to whom you are speaking. Let's say those together three times.

TOGETHER (three times): You, your, yours.

Instructor: Use the pronoun "you" in a sentence for me.
Student: *[gives sentence]*

Instructor: Now say the pronouns "he, she, him, her, it, his, hers, its" together three times.

TOGETHER (three times): He, she, him, her, it, his, hers, its.

Instructor: Use the pronoun "she" in a sentence for me.
Student: *[gives sentence]*

Instructor: The pronouns "we," "us," "our," "ours" mean more than one person. Let's say them together three times.

TOGETHER (three times): We, us, our, ours.

Instructor: Now make up a sentence about you and me. Use the pronoun "we."

Student: *[gives sentence]*

Instructor: The pronouns "They," "them," "their," "theirs" are also used in place of nouns that mean more than one person. You use them when you are talking about a group of people that does not include you! Let's say "They, them, their, theirs" together three times.

TOGETHER (three times): They, them, their, theirs.

Instructor: Make up a sentence using the pronoun "they."
Student: *[gives sentence]*

Instructor: Now I will say the whole list of pronouns for you!

I, me, my, mine;
you, your, yours;
he, she, him, her, it, his, hers, its;
we, us, our, ours;
they, them, their, theirs.

Copywork

Choose one of the following copy assignments.

Emily sang. She sang well.

Don't look, or you will be scared!

Kim and Alex had ice cream. They ate too much!

Enrichment Activity

Have the student write other sentences that use pronouns.

9/18

Verbs (action verbs)
Capitalizing "I"
Copywork: "The baby and I"
Poem review: "The Goops" (Lesson 2)

Note to Instructor: *Review "The Goops" today. Encourage the student to say the poem alone.*

Instructor:	Listen to the definition of a **verb. A verb is a word that does an action, shows a state of being, links two words together, or helps another verb.** Now I want you to repeat parts of this definition after me: **A verb is a word that does an action.**
Student:	*A verb is a word that does an action.*
Instructor:	Now listen to the second part of the definition: **Shows a state of being.** Repeat that for me.
Student:	*Shows a state of being.*
Instructor:	**Links two words together.**
Student:	*Links two words together.*
Instructor:	**Or helps another verb.**
Student:	*Or helps another verb.*
Instructor:	**A verb is a word that does an action.** Let's think of some action verbs together.

Note to Instructor: *Help student to think of action verbs such as: walk, stoop, run, laugh, write, erase, cry, skip, throw, catch, dance, eat, roll, fall, jump, sing, sleep, skate, talk, read, kick, hit, crawl, hop, bark, play, look, paint, climb, swing, float, fly, open, close, move, race, smell, shout, yell, clean, squeak, mew, roar, growl.*

Instructor:	If you were doing these verbs, you would use the word "I" to tell me about it. You would say, "I run," or "I crawl," or "I smell," or "I laugh." You use the word "I" instead of saying your own name. Do you remember what we call a word that takes the place of a noun?
Student:	*A pronoun is a word that takes the place of a noun.*

Note to Instructor: *Prompt student for this definition, if necessary.*

Instructor: The pronoun "I" is always capitalized. I will write "I run" out for you so that you see the capital "I."

Note to Instructor: *Write "I run" and several other "I" sentences, using action verbs, while the student watches. Point out the capital "I" in each sentence.*

Copywork

Choose one of the following sentences.

The baby and I crawl.

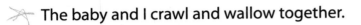 The baby and I crawl and wallow together.

The baby and I crawl, wallow, and giggle together.

9\19

• • • • • • • • • • • • • • • • • • **LESSON 5** • • • • • • • • • • • • • • • • •

Introducing state of being verbs
Copywork: State of being verbs
Poem review: "The Goops" (Lesson 2)

Note to Instructor: *Review "The Goops" today.*

Instructor: **A verb is a word that does an action, shows a state of being, links two words together, or helps another verb.** We have been practicing verbs that do actions. But did you hear in the definition that some verbs show "a state of being"? Let's say, "A verb is a word that does an action or shows a state of being" together three times.

TOGETHER (three times): **A verb is a word that does an action or shows a state of being.**

Instructor: Let's talk about what that means! Some verbs are words that you can do. But some verbs show that you just are! Sit perfectly still for me. You are not jumping, running, crawling, wallowing, or giggling. But you are still here! You just are. Verbs which tell us that something "just is" are called **state of being verbs.** "State of being" means that you are in a state of just being or existing. The state of being verbs are: am, is, are, was, were, be, being, been. I am going to say this list of state of being verbs five times.

Instructor (five times): (Do this in the form of a chant.)
Am [clap]
Is [clap]
Are, was, were [clap]
Be [clap]
Being [clap]
Been [clap] [clap]

Instructor: Now you say them with me five more times.

TOGETHER: (Repeat chant five times, with clapping.)

Instructor: I am going to put some of these state of being verbs in very short sentences that just tell that someone or something exists. These sentences don't tell anything about the person, and they don't tell an action that the person does. These short sentences only say that a person exists. The boy is. The girl is. The man was. The woman was. The people were. Now I will say those sentences to you again. Can you tell me the state of being verb in each sentence?

Instructor: The boy is.
Student: *Is.*

Note to Instructor: *If the student answers "the" or "boy," say the list of state of being verbs again and ask, "Is 'the' in the list?" (etc.) Do not require the student to use a complete sentence— your goal is to have him name the verb only.*

Instructor: The girl is.
Student: *Is.*

Instructor: The man was.
Student: *Was.*

Instructor: The woman was.
Student: *Was.*

Instructor: The people were.
Student: *Were.*

Instructor: Now let's chant our list five more times.

Note to Instructor: *Chant the list with the student five additional times.*

Copywork

Write the following chart on a sheet of paper. Have the student copy it onto his own paper.

<u>State of Being Verbs</u>

    am
    is
    are, was, were.
    be
    being
    been

9/20

State of being verbs

Instructor: **A verb is a word that does an action, shows a state of being, links two words together, or helps another verb.** Let's say, "**A verb is a word that does an action or shows a state of being**" together three times.

TOGETHER (three times): **A verb is a word that does an action or shows a state of being.**

Instructor: Can you name an action verb for me?

Student: *[names an action verb]*

Instructor: You can do an action verb. But a state of being verb just shows that you exist. Let's chant our state of being verbs together five times.

TOGETHER (five times):
Am [clap]
Is [clap]
Are, was, were [clap]
Be [clap]
Being [clap]
Been [clap] [clap]

Instructor: We can combine those state of being verbs with pronouns. Listen:
I am.
He is.
She is.
It is.
We are.
You are.
They are.
I was.
He was.
She was.
It was.
You were.
They were.
Did you hear any action in what I read?

Student: No.

Instructor: All of those sentences used pronouns and state of being verbs. Now I am going say some questions and answers for you. These will show you how state of being verbs can be used without showing action.

Note to Instructor: *Read both the question and the answer, using different voices to pretend that one person asks a question and another answers.*

Instructor: Are you in this room? I am.
Is he in the room with you? He is.
Is your baby sister in bed? She is.
Is your book on the table? It is.
Who is in this room? We are.
Who is with me? You are.
Are other people here? They are.
Who was at lunch? You were.
Who else was at lunch? She was.
Is the delicious sandwich all gone? It is.

Instructor: I just used the state of being verbs "am," "is," "are," "was," and "were." The state of being verbs "be," "being," "been" have to have another verb to help them. We will talk about helping verbs later. Let's say the state of being verbs together one more time.

TOGETHER: Am, is, are, was, were, be, being, been.

Note to Instructor: *Identifying state of being verbs is difficult for many children. This is due to the fact that the verbs "am," "is," "are," "was," "were," "be," "being," and "been" can function as either state of being verbs or, more commonly, as linking verbs. Introduce the concept, but don't worry if the student cannot fully understand it. Distinguishing between linking verbs and state of being verbs is covered in more advanced grammar.*

Enrichment Activity

Have the student make up his own questions and answers. He may ask them to you or to another family member. Remind him that the answers should use pronouns and state of being verbs.

9/23

······· **LESSON 7** ·······

Introducing linking verbs
Poem review: "The Goops" (Lesson 2)

Notes to Instructor: *You will need three light colors of construction paper, glue or tape, and a marker for the enrichment activity. This enrichment activity is strongly recommended to reinforce the lesson on linking verbs.*

Review "The Goops" today.

Today, you will introduce the student to the concept of linking verbs. Linking verbs can connect a pronoun and a noun ("I am a woman"), two nouns ("The woman is President"), a pronoun and an adjective ("I am hungry"), and a noun and an adjective ("The woman is kind"). In the oral exercises that follow, allow the student to select a noun or an adjective to follow the linking verbs. At this point, do not sidetrack him from understanding linking verbs by focusing on the words that follow the linking verb!

Instructor: Last lesson we talked about state of being verbs: am, is, are, was, were, be, being, been. Say those state of being verbs with me three times.

TOGETHER (three times): Am, is, are, was, were, be, being, been.

Instructor: Listen to the definition of a verb: **A verb is a word that does an action, shows a state of being, links two words together, or helps another verb**. Today we're going to talk about the third part of that definition: **Links two words together**. Let's say the verb definition together as far as "**links two words together.**" I will say it first: **A verb is a word that does an action, shows a state of being, or links two words together.** Let's say that together three times.

TOGETHER (three times): **A verb is a word that does an action, shows a state of being, or links two words together.**

Instructor: We have talked about action verbs. Can you give me an action verb?
Student: *[gives action verb]*

Instructor: We have also talked about state of being verbs. State of being verbs just tell us that something exists! In the last lesson, I read you some questions and answers that used state of being verbs. I will repeat them for you.

  Note to Instructor: *Read these again, using different voices for the questions and the answers.*

Instructor: Are you in this room? I am.
  Is he in the room with you? He is.
  Is your baby sister in bed? She is.

Is your book on the table? It is.
Who is in this room? We are.
Who is with me? You are.
Are other people here? They are.
Who was at lunch? You were.
Who else was at lunch? She was.
Is the delicious sandwich all gone? It is.

Instructor: The answers to these questions are very short in order to help you identify state of being verbs. In this lesson you will learn about another type of verb: linking verbs. Most linking verbs are easy to recognize because they are the same verbs as the state of being verbs: am, is, are, was, were, be, being, been. A linking verb links two words together. Do you know how to link hands with someone else? Let's link hands. We are joining hands. Now we are connected together. Do you know what we call the parts of a chain that are joined together?

Note to Instructor: *Wait for response if it is forthcoming, but continue without much delay if the student does not know what to call the parts of a chain.*

Instructor: We call the parts of a chain "links." If people hold hands, we sometimes say they "link" hands. A "link" is something that connects or joins things. Linking verbs can link or connect words together to make interesting sentences. "Am," "is," "are," "was," and "were" are most often used as linking verbs. I will read you a noun and a linking verb and let you complete the sentence. Then the linking verb will connect the noun that I use, with the interesting words that you choose to tell me more about the noun! Here is the first sentence: "The toad was..." Can you tell me what color the toad was?

Student: *The toad was green [or brown].*

Instructor: The linking verb "was" connects "toad" with its color! Can you tell me something about a freight train if I say "The freight train is _____"?

Student: *The freight train is long [or another appropriate word].*

Instructor: The linking verb "is" connects the freight train with the word _____. Now finish this sentence: "Chocolate is..."

Student: *Chocolate is good!*

Instructor: The linking verb "is" connects "chocolate" with "good!" Now can you tell me something about yourself? Begin your sentence with "I am..."

Student: *I am [appropriate noun or adjective].*

Instructor: The linking verb "am" connects the word "I" with a word that tells me more about you! Now finish this sentence: "Dogs are..." What can you tell me about dogs?

Student: *Dogs are [noun or adjective].*

Instructor: The linking verb "are" connects "dogs" with the word that explains more about dogs! Now finish one more sentence for me: "In long ago times, knights in armor were…"

Student: *Knights in armor were [appropriate phrase].*

Instructor: Good job! Now you have used the linking verbs "am," "is," "are," "was," "were" to tell me more about the nouns and pronouns I gave you.

Instructor: Now let's say the state of being verbs we learned last lesson.

TOGETHER: Am, is, are, was, were, be, being, been.

Instructor: Now let's say the linking verbs we learned this lesson. These are the same verbs we just said together!

TOGETHER: Am, is, are, was, were, be, being, been.

Note to Instructor: *Verbs which can serve as either linking or action verbs are: taste, feel, smell, sound, look, appear, become, seem, grow, remain, stay. However, this concept is too advanced for second grade; it will be taught in a later year. (Most grammar books introduce these verbs in late third or early fourth grade.)*

Enrichment Activity

Help the student make a three-link paper chain from three different colors of construction paper that are light enough for the student to clearly see writing on them. The middle link should be yellow or white. While the links are flat, before putting the chain together:

1. Write a linking verb on the yellow or white link.
2. Write a noun or pronoun on another color link.
3. Write an adjective on the third color link. Glue or tape the chain together, showing that the yellow (or white) linking verb "links" the noun or pronoun with the adjective to make a sentence. You could repeat this project writing a noun instead of an adjective for number 3. If possible, look at a real chain and talk about how the links connect or join parts of the chain.

•   **LESSON 8**   • • • • • • • • • • • • • • • • • • •

Linking verbs

Notes to Instructor: *You will need twenty-five index cards and a pen or marker for this lesson. The student will need additional index cards for the enrichment activity.*

On the first five index cards, write the linking verbs (one on each card): am, is, are, was, were.

On eight more cards, write the following words and phrases (one on each card): Dinosaurs, The beach, Goldilocks, Baby kittens, High-speed trains, Candy, Mommy, Caterpillars.

On the last twelve cards, write the following words and phrases (one on each card): ferocious, delicious, cuddly, sandy, fuzzy, cute, thunderously loud, hungry, dangerous, cheerful, purple, tiny.

Help the student to combine the eight "subject cards" (nouns) with the twelve "descriptive cards" (adjectives) using the linking verb cards to connect them. As you form each sentence, point out the linking verb to the student, and remind the student that the linking verb is connecting the two parts of the sentence together.

Enrichment Activity

The student can make up his own nouns and adjectives to assemble into sentences.

9/25

.... **LESSON 9** ....

Story narration: "The Camel's Nose"

Notes to Instructor: *Narration is a skill to be learned through practice. In narration, the student simply tells back a story in his own words. There are two common difficulties in learning to narrate.*

1. The student gives every detail of the story, making the narration too long to write down.

2. The student doesn't know how to start or what to say.

To help young students summarize, we have provided summary questions. After reading the story, ask the student the questions that follow. He should practice answering in complete sentences. If he answers with a phrase or single word, repeat his answer back to him as a complete sentence. Then ask him to repeat that sentence back to you. This begins to train the student to formulate grammatical sentences.

Then ask the student, "What is one thing you remember about the story?" Help him to phrase his answer as a complete sentence. You should then write the sentence down as he watches. Point out any capitalization or punctuation as you write.

If the student uses verbal "fillers" such as "uh," "like," or "you know," encourage him to stop and think in silence until he is ready to speak the sentence. When these "fillers" slip back into the narration, simply repeat what the student has said, omitting the useless word; then have him repeat after you.

There is no rush! This is a skill to be learned. You are training the student in thinking skills, so that he can grasp and retain more knowledge in his later stages of education. Narration exercises train the mind to grasp what is central—an essential skill for note-taking later on.

Read the following story aloud to the student, and then ask the "starter questions" at the end of the story. Remember to encourage the student to answer in complete sentences. Then ask the student, "What is one thing you remember from the story?" Write his answer down and read it back to him.

The Camel's Nose
by Anonymous

A man who lived in the desert bought a favorite pet camel. The camel carried spices, wood, and tents from place to place for the man. Sometimes the man rode on the camel. They made many journeys together.

Every night, the man cooked his supper over a fire, and then set up his tent nearby. The tent was warm—and the desert nights were very cold. One night, the camel stuck just his nose in the opening of the tent. "Master," said the camel, "my nose is a little bit cold. If I could put just my nose inside your tent, I would sleep better." "Yes," said the man, "the tent is large enough for your nose. You may put your nose into the tent." So the camel stuck his nose under the front flap of the tent.

Not long after, the camel said, "Good master, thank you for letting me put my nose into the tent. My nose is beautifully warm! But the rest of my head would like to be near you, too." The man thought, "My camel is too large to come into this tent. But his head is small! He can put his head into my tent." So he said, "Of course. You may put your whole head into my tent." The camel wriggled his head into the tent. But, very soon, the camel said, "Kind Master, I may catch cold if my head is warm and my body is cold. May I please put my neck inside, too?" The camel's request seemed reasonable, so the man said, "You may put your neck in the tent, too."

After a little while, the camel said, "Generous master, I am tired of standing here. May I kneel with my front legs in the tent?" The master did not want his animal exhausted in the morning, so he moved over and allowed the camel to put his nose, his head, his neck, and his front legs inside the tent.

The man was beginning to fall asleep when he heard, "Wonderful master, I do not want you to be uncomfortable in the night and I worry that when I kneel this way, half-in and half-out of the tent, cold air rushes into your tent. Perhaps I should come all the way in, so that you can close the flaps behind me."

The man agreed, and he opened the tent flaps for the camel to come inside. But when the camel was in the tent all the way, the camel said, "We have a problem. The tent is too small for us both to lie down and sleep. I think it would be better if you went outside to sleep." And with that, the camel pushed his master out of the tent and would not let him back in.

While shivering outside in the cold, the man thought to himself, "I should never have let the camel put his nose into the tent! I didn't think his nose was a bad thing—but if I had stopped his nose from coming in, the rest of him would not have followed! And I would still be in my warm bed."

Note to Instructor: *Use these questions to help the student summarize the story:*

Instructor: Why did the camel want to put his nose into the tent?
Student: *The camel's nose was cold.*

Instructor: What did the camel want to do after his nose was inside the tent?
Student: *He wanted to put his head into the tent.*

Instructor: What did the camel want to do next?
Student: *He wanted to put his neck inside the tent.*

Instructor: Why did the man let the whole camel inside the tent?
Student: *The man wanted to close the tent flaps to keep out the cold air.*

Instructor: Once the camel was inside, what did he tell the man to do?
Student: *He told the man to go outside the tent so that he would have room to sleep.*

Note to Instructor: *Use the following information as a guide for discussion if you wish.*

Bad habits are things that should be stopped before they get started and crowd out good habits. What are some bad habits that it would be good to stop before they are too hard to break?

Bad friends are another thing that should be stopped before they get started. Little by little, bad company can crowd out good companions. What can you do to prevent bad companions from taking over your time?

LESSON 10

Linking verbs

Note to Instructor: *The student will need thirteen index cards for the enrichment activity.*

Instructor: I will say the definition of a verb for you: **A verb is a word that does an action, shows a state of being, links two words together, or helps another verb**. We have learned about action verbs, state of being verbs, and linking verbs. Let's say the first three parts of the definition together three times. I will say it first: **A verb is a word that does an action, shows a state of being, or links two words together**.

TOGETHER: **A verb is a word that does an action, shows a state of being, or links two words together**.

Instructor: Listen to the following sentences from "The Camel's Nose." Each sentence has a linking verb in it.

The tent was warm.
The desert nights were very cold.
My nose is a little bit cold.
The tent is large enough for your nose.
My nose is beautifully warm!
My camel is too large to come into this tent.
But his head is small!
The tent is too small for us both.

Now I will read you each sentence again. Can you find the linking verb in each sentence?

Note to Instructor: *Help the student identify the verbs "is," "was," and "were" in each sentence.*

Instructor: Now let's find the words that the verbs link together. In "The tent was warm," what was warm?

Student: *The tent was warm.*

Instructor: "Was" links "tent" and "warm" together. Now you know more about the tent. What were the desert nights like?

Student: *The desert nights were very cold.*

Instructor: The linking verb "were" links "the desert nights" together with "very cold." In the sentence "The tent is large enough for your nose," what word links "The tent" with the description "large enough for your nose"?

Student:	*The word "is."*
Instructor:	"Is" is a linking verb. The next sentence is "My nose is beautifully warm!" What does "beautifully warm" describe?
Student:	*"Beautifully warm" describes "my nose."*
Instructor:	What word links "my nose" to "beautifully warm?"
Student:	*The word "is" links "my nose" to "beautifully warm."*
Instructor:	Can you use a linking verb to connect these two phrases? "The tent" and "too small for us both."
Student:	*The tent is too small for us both.*

Enrichment Activity

Ask the student to write the following words and phrases on separate index cards (you can help with the longer phrases). When the cards are finished, ask the student to assemble the sentences properly.

The tent

was

warm

My nose

is

a little bit cold

large enough for your nose

beautifully warm

My camel

too large to come into this tent

But his head

small

too small for us both.

9/27

•   **LESSON 11**   • • • • • • • • • • • • • • • •

Beginning poem booklet
Copywork: "The Year"
Poem review: "The Goops" (Lesson 2)

Notes to Instructor: *The student will need art supplies and either two pieces of construction paper or a folder.*

Review "The Goops" today.

Over the course of the next twenty lessons, the student will make pages for a booklet titled "The Year." He will need thirteen sheets of lined paper for this project, as well as construction paper or a folder to use for a cover.

Instructor: Today we are going to read a poem about the twelve months of the year. The poem begins with January, the first month of the year. January is a winter month. The season of winter officially begins on December 21, but January 1 is considered the first day of the year. I will read the poem to you. Follow along as I move my finger beneath the words.

The Year
By Sara Coleridge, adapted by Sara Buffington

January brings the snow,

Helps the skis and sleds to go.
Makes our feet and fingers glow

February brings the rain,

Thaws the frozen lake again.

March brings breezes loud and shrill,
To stir
Stirs the dancing daffodil.

April brings the primrose sweet,

Scatters daisies at our feet.

May brings sunshine full and bright,

Sends the busy bees to flight.

May brings flocks of
pretty lambs
Skipping by their
fleecy dams

22

June brings tulips, lilies, roses,

Fills the children's hands with posies.

Hot July brings stormy showers,

Lemonade, and lazy hours. *Apricots and gillyflowers*

August brings the warmest air, *sheaves of corn*

Sandy feet and sea-wet hair. *Then the harvest home is borne.*

Warm September brings the fruit; Sportsmen then begin to shoot

September brings the fruit so sweet,

Apples ripe from summer heat.

Fresh October brings the pheasant Then to gather nuts is pleasant

October brings the colored trees,

Scampering squirrels and cooling breeze.

Dull November brings the blast,

Then the leaves are whirling fast.

Chill December brings the sleet,

Blazing fire, and Christmas treat.[1]

1 An alternate last line: "Blazing fire, and winter treat."

Copywork

On one sheet of lined paper, have the student copy the title of the poem "The Year." Help him center the title (this will serve as his title page). Remind him that each word in the title begins with a capital letter. Have him illustrate a folder or piece of construction paper to serve as the booklet's cover. You will assemble the booklet when he has copied all twelve verses.

If you live in a location where the seasons are so different that the poem has little meaning for the student, you do not have to use this poem. Instead, substitute a sentence you write for the student (poetry is not necessary!) describing something that happens each month of the year in your area. The student will copy your sentences instead of the above verses in his "The Year" book.

Enrichment Activity

Have the student make two-line rhyming couplets about one or more months and substitute these couplets for the suggested poem. Have a family or group poetry composing session in which everyone contributes ideas.

•   **LESSON 12**   •

Four types of sentences
Seasons
Copywork: "January"

Note to Instructor: *The student will need art supplies or old magazines for winter pictures.*

Instructor: In the poem we read last lesson, we read statements about the months. We read that "February brings the rain," and that "April brings the primrose sweet." Those are **sentences. A sentence is a group of words that expresses a complete thought.** Let's say that definition together three times.

TOGETHER (three times): **A sentence is a group of words that expresses a complete thought.**

Instructor: **A sentence begins with a capital letter and ends with a punctuation mark.** Let's say that together three times.

TOGETHER (three times): **A sentence begins with a capital letter and ends with a punctuation mark.**

Instructor: There are four different types of sentences. **A statement gives information.** Repeat that definition for me.

Student: *A statement gives information.*

Instructor: Here are some statements. December, January, and February are winter months. March, April, and May are spring months. Both of those sentences give you information. The second type of sentence is a command. **A command gives an order or makes a request.** Let's say that together three times.

TOGETHER (three times): **A command gives an order or makes a request.**

Instructor: Suppose it were August. August is a summer month. I might command you, "Go play in the snow!" Would you be able to do it?

Student: *No!*

Instructor: What if I made the command a request? Please, go get me an icicle! Could you do it then?

Student: *No!*

Instructor: It is too hot for snow and icicles during June, July, and August. They are all summer months. The third type of sentence is a question. **A question asks something.** Is September a fall month?

Student:	*Yes.*
Instructor:	Did I just ask you a question?
Student:	*Yes.*

Instructor: Did you answer yes? I keep asking you questions! I am asking you for information. You can make a statement in answer to my question. You can say "September is a fall month." There is one more type of sentence left—an exclamation. If I were to say "The fall colors are spectacular!" with sudden, strong emotion, that would be an exclamation. **An exclamation shows sudden or strong feeling.** It ends with an exclamation point. Say that with me: **An exclamation shows sudden or strong feeling.**

TOGETHER: **An exclamation shows sudden or strong feeling.**

Instructor: Now we have reviewed the four types of sentences. They are statement, command, question, exclamation. Say that with me twice.

TOGETHER (twice): Statement, command, question, exclamation.

Copywork

Have the student copy the January couplet from the poem "The Year" (Lesson 11) onto a blank sheet of lined paper. If the student has great difficulty copying both lines of the couplet, have him copy one line and you write the second line for him. He can illustrate the paper by drawing a picture of a January activity (sledding, building a snowman). If he prefers, he can cut pictures from a magazine and paste them onto the page.

Enrichment Activity

Have the student come up with his own statements, questions, commands, and exclamations. He can write these down, or simply say them orally.

10/1

•   **LESSON 13**   • • • • • • • • • • • • • • • • • • •

Commas (dates and addresses)
Copywork: "February"

Note to Instructor: *The student will need art supplies or old magazines for winter pictures.*

Instructor: The poem that you are working on lists the proper names of all of the months. In which month were you born? Write that month on your paper.

Note to Instructor: *Help the student to spell his birthday month correctly. Remind him that it should begin with a capital letter.*

Instructor: On what day of that month were you born? Write that day now. In what year were you born? Write that year next. This is the date of your birthday. When we write a date, we put a comma between the day of the month and the year.

Note to Instructor: *Help the student to write the date of his birthday correctly.*

Instructor: Let's practice writing another date correctly. We will write today's date: the month, the day, a comma, and then the year.

Note to Instructor: *Help the student write today's date correctly.*

Instructor: We use a comma whenever we need to separate two words or numbers. The comma that separates the day from the year helps you to keep those two numbers apart. Otherwise, you might think they were all one long number! We also use a comma to separate the name of a city from the name of a state. Otherwise, you might think that they were one long name! I will write out the name of our city and state for you.

Note to Instructor: *Write the name of your city and state for the student. Point out the comma that separates them.*

Instructor: Your city and state are part of your address. I will write the rest of your address for you now. Then you will copy it, putting commas where they belong.

Note to Instructor: *Write the student's address neatly. Ask him to copy it. Point out any commas in the address.*

Instructor: Your birthday is the special day on which you were born, and your address is the special place where you live! Both of these have commas in them.

Copywork

Have the student copy the February couplet from the poem "The Year" (Lesson 11) onto a blank sheet of lined paper. If the student has great difficulty copying both lines of the couplet, have him copy one line and you write the second line. He can illustrate the paper by drawing a picture of a February activity (perhaps one that has to do with a holiday: Presidents' Day, Valentine's Day). If he prefers, he can cut pictures from a magazine and paste them onto the page.

10/2

• • • • • • • • • • • • • • • LESSON 14 • • • • • • • • • • • • • • •

Commas in a series
Copywork: "Snuggles, wiggles, grins, and giggles"
Poem review: "The Goops" (Lesson 2)

Note to Instructor: *Review "The Goops" today.*

Instructor: We put a comma between a city and a state. We also put one between the day and the year in a date. Commas separate words! You can also separate words by using "and." If I were to give you a cookie, I could also give you milk to go with it. I could say, "I will give you a cookie and milk." The "and" comes between the cookie and the milk. But if I were also to give you an apple and a napkin, the list of things I am giving you is beginning to get long! I would have to say, "I will give you a cookie and milk and an apple and a napkin." Instead of putting "and" between each one of those items, I can just put a comma between them! I will put a comma after every item I am giving you—except for the last one at the end of the sentence. It has a period after it! Now I can say, "I will give you a cookie [COMMA] milk [COMMA] an apple [COMMA] and a napkin [PERIOD]"

Note to Instructor: *Read these sentences to the student just as written. Then, show the student the written sentences below.*

I will give you a cookie and milk and an apple and a napkin.

I will give you a cookie, milk, an apple, and a napkin.

Instructor: Whenever you separate items in a series by putting a comma after each one, you should keep the very last "and." "Series" is another word for "list." Listen to me read these series and follow along as I move my finger under the words.

Note to Instructor: *Pause as you come to each comma.*

I am going to play baseball. I need a ball, a bat, a glove, and a helmet.

I am going to make cookies. I will use flour, sugar, butter, vanilla, and eggs.

I went to the zoo. I saw tigers, elephants, lions, monkeys, and snakes.

Instructor: These lists have commas after each item. In each list, the word "and" comes before the last item. Read the following sentences to me.

Note to Instructor: *Have the student read the following pairs of sentences from the book.*

Tables are set with plates and bowls and glasses and cups.

Tables are set with plates, bowls, glasses, and cups.

My art work is done with pencils and crayons and paints.

My art work is done with pencils, crayons, and paints.

Parts of my body are hands and arms and legs.

Parts of my body are hands, arms, and legs.

Instructor: Items in a list should be separated by commas.

Copywork

Choose one of the following copy exercises:

A baby can yell, smile, and sleep.

My pet can run, growl, play, escape, and bite!

My little sister snuggles, wiggles, grins, and giggles.

• • • • • • • • • • • • • • • • • • **LESSON 15** • • • • • • • • • • • • • • • •

Introducing helping verbs
Copywork: "March"

10/3

Note to Instructor: *The student will need art supplies or old magazines for spring pictures.*

Instructor: **A verb is a word that does an action, shows a state of being, links two words together, or helps another verb.** Let's say, "**A verb is a word that does an action, shows a state of being, links two words together, or helps another verb**" three times.

TOGETHER (three times): **A verb is a word that does an action, shows a state of being, links two words together, or helps another verb.**

Instructor: Can you name an action verb for me?

Student: *[names an action verb]*

Instructor: You can do an action verb. But a state of being verb just shows that you exist. Let's chant our state of being verbs together five times.

TOGETHER (five times):
>Am [clap]
>Is [clap]
>Are, was, were [clap]
>Be [clap]
>Being [clap]
>Been [clap] [clap]

Instructor: These verbs can also function as linking verbs. These linking verbs link two words together: "She is happy," or "The mother was glad to see her little boy!" Now it's time for us to talk about that last part of the verb definition: A verb can help another verb. Say that with me three times:

TOGETHER (three times): A verb can help another verb.

Instructor: Listen to this sentence: "The camel was pushing his way into the tent." The camel was doing something active. What was he doing?

Student: *He was pushing.*

Instructor: But if I just said "The camel pushing his way into the tent," that would sound odd! "Pushing" needs another verb to help it. The verb "was" is helping the verb "pushing." Together, they make sense. "The camel was pushing his way into the tent." Do you recognize the verb "was"? You have learned that it can act as either a state of being verb or a linking verb. The verbs "am," "is," "are," "was," "were," "be," "being," and "been" can help action verbs to get their job done. Let's repeat those verbs.

TOGETHER: Am, is, are, was, were, be, being, been.

Instructor: Now I am also going to add some other helping verbs:
Have, has, had [clap]
Do, does, did [clap]
Shall, will, should, would, may, might, must [clap] [clap]
Can, could!

That is a very long list, but you have already found out that you can learn lots of long things if you just say them enough times. So that is what we will do today and for other days to come. I will say it three more times.

Am [clap]
Is [clap]
Are, was, were [clap]
Be [clap]
Being [clap]
Been [clap] [clap]
Have, has, had [clap]
Do, does, did [clap]
Shall, will, should, would, may, might, must [clap] [clap]
Can, could!

Instructor: Listen to this sentence: "A man who was living in the desert bought a pet camel." Repeat that sentence for me.

Student: *A man who was living in the desert bought a pet camel.*

Instructor: Now listen: "A man who living in the desert bought a pet camel." I left a word out. Do you know what word I left out?

Note to Instructor: *Repeat both versions of the sentence until the student can identify the missing "was."*

Instructor: "Was" is a helping verb. The verb "living" has to have the helping verb "was" with it, or else it doesn't make sense! What action verb comes after the helping verb "was"?

Student: *Living.*

Instructor: "Was" and "living" are both verbs. "Living" is the action verb and "was" is the helping verb. There is another action word in this sentence, too. What action had the man done to get a camel?

Student: *The man bought a camel.*

Instructor: "Bought" is a verb that shows action. But the action verb "bought" doesn't need a helping verb with it. Listen to the next sentence: "The camel carried spices and wood for the man." What is the action verb in this sentence?

Student: *Carried.*

Note to Instructor: *Give the student any necessary help to identify the action verb.*

Instructor: "Carried" doesn't need a helping verb either. But listen to this next sentence: "Sometimes the man would ride on the camel." Listen to it again: "Sometimes the man would ride on the camel." Now listen one more time: "Sometimes the man ride on the camel." What word did I leave out?

Student: *Would.*

Instructor: The action verb "ride" needs the helping verb "would" in this sentence. Without the helping verb, it doesn't sound right! Now I will say the whole list of helping verbs for you again. Listen carefully:
Am [clap]
Is [clap]
Are, was, were [clap]
Be [clap]
Being [clap]
Been [clap] [clap]
Have, has, had [clap]
Do, does, did [clap]
Shall, will, should, would, may, might, must [clap] [clap]
Can, could!

Note to Instructor: *Repeat this list for the student three more times.*

Copywork

Have the student copy the March couplet from the poem "The Year" (Lesson 11) onto a blank sheet of lined paper. If the student has great difficulty copying both lines of the couplet, have him copy one line and you write the second line. He can illustrate the paper by drawing a picture of a March activity (perhaps one involving wind or kites—see the Enrichment Activity, below). If he prefers, he can cut pictures from a magazine and paste them onto the page.

Enrichment Activity

Have the student read, illustrate, or memorize the following poem about wind.

The Wind

By Robert Louis Stevenson

I saw you toss the kites on high
And blow the birds about the sky;
And all around I heard you pass,
Like ladies' skirts across the grass—
 O wind, a-blowing all day long,
 O wind, that sings so loud a song!

I saw the different things you did,
But always you yourself you hid.
I felt you push, I heard you call,
I could not see yourself at all—
 O wind, a-blowing all day long,
 O wind, that sings so loud a song!

O you, that are so strong and cold,
O blower, are you young or old?
Are you a beast of field and tree,
Or just a stronger child than me?
 O wind, a-blowing all day long,
 O wind, that sings so loud a song!

••••••••••••••••••• **LESSON 16** ••••••••••••••••••

Noun review
Verb review
Copywork: "April"

10|9

Note to Instructor: *The student will need art supplies and old magazines for spring pictures.*

Instructor: Let's review what a noun is. Say after me: **A noun is the name of a person, place, thing, or idea.**

Student: *A noun is the name of a person, place, thing, or idea.*

Instructor: I am going to give the common name of a person, place, or thing, and I want you to give me a special, proper name for each. Here is a common name for a person: girl. Now, can you give me the special, proper name of a girl?

Student: *[the proper name of a real girl]*

Instructor: "State." That is a common noun that names a place—there are many states. Can you give me the proper name of our state?

Student: *[name of state]*

Instructor: "Cereal" is a common noun. Can you think of the proper name of a cereal that you like?

Student: *[Cheerios or some other cereal name]*

Instructor: We will talk only about common nouns for ideas. Remember that an idea is something you can think about in your mind, but can't see or touch. I'll tell you one idea and you try to remember others we have talked about. I'm thinking about the idea noun "excitement." Can you think of another noun that names an idea?

Student: *[possible answers: happiness, joy, freedom, sadness, fear, etc.]*

Instructor: Remember, proper nouns always begin with capital letters. Your name is a proper noun, because there is only one you! Write your full proper name on your paper now.

Note to Instructor: *As the student writes, remind him to begin his names with capital letters. Help him to write his first, middle, and last names.*

Instructor: Nouns are one kind of word. Verbs are a different kind of word. I will say the definition of a verb for you: **A verb is a word that does an action, shows a state of being, links two words together, or helps another verb.** Let's say, **"A verb is a word that does an action, shows a state of being, links two words together, or helps another verb"** three times.

TOGETHER (three times): **A verb is a word that does an action, shows a state of being, links two words together, or helps another verb.**

Instructor: We have learned about action verbs, state of being verbs, linking verbs, and helping verbs. We learned a whole list of helping verbs. I will say them for you now:
Am [clap]
Is [clap]
Are, was, were [clap]
Be [clap]
Being [clap]
Been [clap] [clap]
Have, has, had [clap]
Do, does, did [clap]
Shall, will, should, would, may, might, must [clap] [clap]
Can, could!

Let's recite that list together three times.

TOGETHER (three times):
Am [clap]
Is [clap]
Are, was, were [clap]
Be [clap]
Being [clap]
Been [clap] [clap]
Have, has, had [clap]
Do, does, did [clap]
Shall, will, should, would, may, might, must [clap] [clap]
Can, could!

Instructor: I will read you some sentences where some nouns are doing some action verbs! Each action verb has a helping verb with it. We will find the action verb and then talk about which word helps it.

Instructor: "The bullfrog was leaping from lily pad to lily pad." Who or what was leaping?
Student: *The bullfrog was leaping.*

Instructor: "Bullfrog" is the name of an animal. It is a noun. What was the bullfrog doing?
Student: *The bullfrog was leaping.*

Instructor: If I say "The bullfrog leaping," that doesn't make sense! What word did I leave out? I left out the word "was." "Was" is a helping verb that helps the verb "leap." Now I will read you another sentence: "The pigs were wallowing in a huge puddle of gooey mud." Who or what was wallowing?

Student:	The pigs were wallowing.

Instructor:	"Pigs" is a noun. What were the pigs doing?
Student:	The pigs were wallowing.

Instructor:	Does it sound right if I just say "The pigs wallowing in a huge puddle of gooey mud"?
Student:	No.

Instructor:	What word helps the verb "wallowing"?
Student:	Were.

Instructor:	"The garbage truck is rattling down the street." Who or what is rattling?
Student:	The garbage truck.

Instructor:	"Truck" is a noun. It is the name of a thing. What is the truck doing?
Student:	The garbage truck is rattling down the street.

Instructor:	What helping verb goes along with the verb "rattling"?
Student:	Is.

Instructor:	Good! I will say the list of helping verbs to you one more time. Am, is, are, was, were. Be, being, been. Have, has, had, do, does, did. Shall, will, should, would, may, might, must, can, could.

Copywork

Have the student copy the April couplet from the poem "The Year" (Lesson 11) onto a blank sheet of lined paper. If the student has great difficulty copying both lines of the couplet, have him copy one line and you write the second line. He can illustrate the paper by drawing a picture of something he would observe or celebrate in April (flowers, a religious holiday). If he prefers, he can cut this picture from a magazine and paste it onto the page.

Enrichment Activity

Help the student to make up sentences that use helping verbs to help out action verbs.

10/10

.... LESSON 17 ....

Capitalization (proper names, initials, titles of respect, addresses, poems)

Notes to Instructor: *You will need five index cards for the enrichment activity.*

Chant the helping verb list three times with the student:
Am, is, are, was, were.
Be, being, been.
Have, has, had, do, does, did.
Shall, will, should, would, may, might, must, can, could.

Instructor: Today we are going to review capital letters. What is your full name?

Student: *[gives full name]*

Instructor: Each of your names begins with a capital letter because your names are your special, proper names. And you have learned that proper nouns begin with capital letters. Let's say that I want to put your name on something that belongs to you—maybe a ball you take to the playground, or a toy you take to the beach, or a coat that looks just like your friend's coat. But I don't want to write out all of your names. Do you know how I could do that? I could write just the first letter of each of your names. Remember, we call the first letter of a proper name its initial. The word "initial" means "first" or "beginning." The initial letter of a proper noun is always a capital letter. What is the first letter of your first name?

Student: *[initial letter of first name]*

Instructor: What is the first letter of your middle name?

Student: *[initial letter of middle name]*

Instructor: What is the initial letter of your last name?

Student: *[initial letter of last name]*

Instructor: Now, I want you to write your initials. When we write initials, we capitalize each one. We also put a period after each initial.

Student: *[writes initials]*

Note to Instructor: *Assist as necessary.*

Instructor: Initials are a short way to write a word. There are other kinds of words that we also write in a short way. Instead of writing the whole word, we only write two or three letters of the word. We call this "abbreviating" or "shortening" a word. Titles of respect, like Mr., Mrs., Miss, and Dr., show we respect the position of a person. When these titles are written, they are often abbreviated. I am going to show you the abbreviated (short) way to write some common titles of respect.

Note to Instructor: *Have the student watch you write—one at a time— the following abbreviations for titles of respect and the titles for which the abbreviations stand. As you write each one, say the word aloud and show the student that each starts with a capital letter and ends with a period (except for "Miss"). As you write, form lists in two columns so you can alternate covering the columns for a practice exercise.*

Mr.	Mister	man
Dr.	Doctor	man or woman
Mrs.	Mistress	married woman
—	Miss	unmarried woman
Ms.	—	can refer to any woman

Instructor: I want you to copy each of these abbreviations and say the word for which it stands. Notice that "Miss" is not an abbreviation.

Student: *[copies each abbreviation and pronounces the word for which it stands]*

Instructor: The words for "street," "avenue" and "road" are often abbreviated as well.

Note to Instructor: *Have the student watch you write —one at a time— the following abbreviations and the words for which they stand. If your address contains any abbreviation other than those below, include it in the list. Copy the following abbreviations and the words for which they stand in two columns so you can alternate covering the columns for a practice exercise.*

Instructor: I want you to copy these words and their abbreviations.

Student: *[copies the lists]*

St.	street
Rd.	road
Ave.	avenue

Instructor: All of the abbreviations we have written today begin with a capital letter because they stand for the special, proper name of a person or a place. The names of states are abbreviated in a special way. Each state has a two-letter abbreviation. Both letters are capitalized, and there is no period after them. State abbreviations break all the rules! The post office wants everyone to write their state abbreviation in the same way so that the machines that sort the mail can read the addresses easily. Here is the abbreviation for our state.

Note to Instructor: *Write out the full name of your state and its postal abbreviation. Ask the student to copy both the name and the abbreviation.*

Instructor: Before we finish today's lesson, I want to review one more rule about capital letters. Capitalize titles and the beginning of every line in poetry. Let's look back at the poem "The Wind" in Lesson 15. Both words in the title are capitalized. Can you point to the capital letter that begins each line?

Instructor: Now I would like you to repeat each one of these capitalization rules after me. Proper names begin with capital letters.

Student: *Proper names begin with capital letters.*

Instructor: When we write initials, we capitalize each one.

Student: *When we write initials, we capitalize each one.*

Instructor: Initials are followed by periods.

Student: *Initials are followed by periods.*

Instructor: Abbreviated titles of respect are capitalized and followed by periods.

Student: *Abbreviated titles of respect are capitalized and followed by periods.*

Instructor: Remember, we don't put a period after the title "Miss." Capitalize titles and the beginning of every line in poetry.

Student: *Capitalize titles and the beginning of every line in poetry.*

Enrichment Activity

On five cards, copy the titles of respect on one side and the words for which they stand on the other side. The student may use these to practice saying and writing titles of respect in proper form. This same activity may be used for other abbreviations.

10/15

• • • • • • • • • • • • • • • • • • • **LESSON 18** • • • • • • • • • • • • • • • • • •

Introducing picture narration: "Dick and Lawless in Holyrood Forest" by N. C. Wyeth

Note to Instructor: *Like story narration, picture narration allows the young student to practice oral composition without forcing him to invent a topic. Picture narration also improves observation skills.*

Ask the following questions to help the student describe the picture. Remember to encourage the student to answer in complete sentences. If necessary, repeat fragmentary answers in the form of a complete sentence and then ask the student to repeat the complete sentence back to you. ("What time of year is it in the picture?" "Winter." "Say that after me: It is winter in the picture.") Sample answers are provided, but any answer based on the picture is acceptable.

Instructor: Look at the picture while I tell you about the artist, Newell Convers Wyeth. He was born in 1882 in Massachusetts and spent his life illustrating classic books such as *Robin Hood* and *Treasure Island*. He painted this picture to illustrate *The Black Arrow*, an adventure written by Robert Louis Stevenson. The two men in the picture, the hero and his friend, are trying to get through a forest without being spotted by their enemies.

What time of year is it in the picture?
Student: *It is winter.*

Instructor: What two things tell you that it is winter?
Student: *There is snow on the ground, and the leaves are off the tree.*

Instructor: Do you think it is night or daytime?
Student: *It is night. [Either answer is acceptable, but if the student answers "daytime," ask him why.]*

Instructor: What month could it be?
Student: *[Any month during which snow might be on the ground is acceptable.]*

Instructor: What are the men carrying?
Student: *One is carrying a spear and the other is carrying a bow.*

Instructor: What are the men wearing? List at least three things.
Student: *The men are wearing hoods, gloves, boots, and jackets.*

Instructor: The man with the spear is looking for a path through the snow. What is the other man doing?
Student: *He is looking behind them for enemies.*

Instructor: Enemies could follow the two men easily in the snow. Why?
Student: *The men are leaving tracks.*

Note to Instructor: *You can view this painting and others from* The Black Arrow *in the Brandwine River Museum N. C. Wyeth collection. Visit http://brandywine.doetech.net/results.cfm?ParentID=126881 or search for "Black Arrow" at http://brandywine.doetech.net.*

· · · · · · · · · · · · · · · · · · · **LESSON 19** · · · · · · · · · · · · · · · · · · ·

Contractions
Copywork: Contractions

Note to Instructor: *The student will need a highlighter marker.*

Chant the helping verb list three times with the student:

Am [clap]
Is [clap]
Are, was, were [clap]
Be [clap]
Being [clap]
Been [clap] [clap]
Have, has, had [clap]
Do, does, did [clap]
Shall, will, should, would, may, might, must [clap] [clap]
Can, could!

Instructor: We have already studied initials and abbreviations. Initials and abbreviations are two ways to shorten a word. Today we will talk about another way to shorten words— contractions. **A contraction is made up of two words put together into one word with some letters left out.** A punctuation mark called an apostrophe is put in the place of the missing letters.

Note to Instructor: *Write the contractions "I'm" and "you're," showing the student how to make an apostrophe. Continue to write as directed in the dialogue below.*

Instructor: The contraction "I'm" is a short way of saying "I am." Instead of saying "I am hungry," you might say "I'm hungry." First, I will write "I am" for you. Then, I will write them together: "Iam." That looks funny, doesn't it? When we put the words "I" and "am" together, we leave out the "a" and put an apostrophe in its place to show that a letter has been left out. Now I will write the contraction properly: "I'm." Repeat this sentence after me: "I am learning to speak properly."

Student: *I am learning to speak properly.*

Instructor: Now use the contraction "I'm" instead of "I am."

Student: *I'm learning to speak properly.*

Instructor: "You are" can be contracted into "You're." I will write both of those out for you. Can you show me which letter has been left out?

Note to Instructor: *Write "You are" on the paper, and then write "You're" directly underneath it.*

Student: *The letter "a."*

Instructor: The apostrophe takes the place of the "a."

Note to Instructor: *Repeat for the following set of contractions, writing each contraction directly underneath the full form of the word so that the student can see which letter or letters have been replaced by the apostrophe.*

He is	She is	It is	We will	You are
He's	She's	It's	We'll	You're

I cannot	He does not	They were not
I can't	He doesn't	They weren't

Copywork

Title a paper "Contractions." Have the student copy the following list:

He is	She is	It is	We will	You are
He's	She's	It's	We'll	You're

With a colored marker, have the student highlight letters in the first row that were left out in the second. Save this sheet and add to it in the next lesson.

·   **LESSON 20**   ·

Contractions
Copywork: Contractions

Note to Instructor: *The student will need a highlighter marker.*

Instructor: **A contraction is made up of two words put together into one word with some letters left out.** A punctuation mark called an apostrophe is put in the place of the missing letters. Today I will say some sentences that do not use contractions. I want you to try to say the sentence back to me, using the correct contraction. For example, I will say "I cannot wait until lunch!" And you will say back to me "I can't wait for lunch!" "Can't" is the contraction for "cannot."

Note to Instructor: *Prompt the student if he cannot identify the correct contraction.*

Instructor: He is going to ride the subway home.
Student: *He's going to ride the subway home.*

Instructor: She is hoping to find a quarter under one of the seats.
Student: *She's hoping to find a quarter under one of the seats.*

Instructor: It is hidden down beneath the cushion.
Student: *It's hidden down beneath the cushion.*

Instructor: They will buy a piece of candy if they find the quarter.
Student: *They'll buy a piece of candy if they find the quarter.*

Instructor: She said, "I cannot find the quarter!"
Student: *She said, "I can't find the quarter!"*

Instructor: He said, "I will try!"
Student: *He said, "I'll try!"*

Instructor: And then they found the quarter and bought candy with it. There aren't any contractions in that sentence! But I just used one—"aren't." What do you think "aren't" is short for?

Note to Instructor: *Help the student identify "aren't" as a contraction for "are not."*

Instructor: We use contractions when we speak and when we write stories and friendly letters. But usually, contractions are not used in formal writing like compositions and business letters.

Copywork

Have the student copy the following list onto the "Contractions" page begun in the last lesson.

I cannot	He does not	They were not
I can't	He doesn't	They weren't

With a highlighter marker, have the student highlight letters in the first row that were left out in the second.

Enrichment Activity

Cover the contractions row and have the student try writing each contraction from memory by looking at the two words from which the contraction is made.

•••••••••••••••• LESSON 21 ••••••••••••••••

Contractions using "not"
Copywork: "May"

Note to Instructor: *The student will need art supplies or old magazines for spring pictures, as well as construction paper for the enrichment activity.*

Instructor: **A contraction is made up of two words put together into one word with some letters left out.** I am going to show you a list of today's contractions. They all end with the same letters.

Note to Instructor: *Show the student the following list.*

aren't	shouldn't
weren't	couldn't
hasn't	wouldn't
haven't	don't
doesn't	can't
didn't	isn't
won't	

Instructor: If we wrote out the words that make up these contractions, you would see that the same word would end every phrase. Can you tell what it would be?

Student: *They all end with the word "not."*

Instructor: When you write a contraction with "not," you put the words together with no space or punctuation mark between them. Then you put an apostrophe in the place of the "o" in "not."

Note to Instructor: *Write "would not" on your paper. Then write "wouldnot." Then, erase the "o" in "not" and substitute an apostrophe. Do the same for "did not" and "were not."*

Instructor: In some of these contractions, other letters disappear too! "Will not" is written "won't." What letters have disappeared? One letter has changed! Can you tell which one?

Note to Instructor: *Write "will not" and then write "won't" beneath it. Point out that the "i" has changed to an "o" and that each "l" has disappeared, as well as the "o" in "not"!*

Instructor: You don't have to memorize any rules about these contractions. You probably already know these words! I will say the full forms of the words, and you can tell me whether you know the contraction that goes with them.

Note to Instructor: *Read the following list to the student. Wait for the student to respond with the appropriate contraction. Prompt him if he is unable to think of it.*

are not	aren't
were not	weren't
has not	hasn't
have not	haven't
does not	doesn't
did not	didn't
should not	shouldn't
could not	couldn't
would not	wouldn't
do not	don't
cannot	can't
is not	isn't
will not	won't

Copywork

Have the student copy the May couplet from the poem "The Year" (Lesson 11) onto a blank sheet of lined paper. If the student has great difficulty copying both lines of the couplet, have him copy one line and you write the second line. He can illustrate the paper by drawing a picture of something he would observe or celebrate in May (birds, spring picnics, Memorial Day, Mother's Day, or another holiday that your family celebrates). If he prefers, he can cut pictures from a magazine and paste them onto the page.

Enrichment Activity

Have the student make a Mother's Day card. Even if it isn't Mother's Day, Mother will appreciate the card!

Lesson 22

·   **LESSON 22**   · · · · · · · · · · · · · · · · · ·

Introducing dictation: "March"

Note to Instructor: *Now that the student has practiced copying, it is time to move on to dictation. Copying teaches the student the conventions of written language. Now you will begin to use dictation as a teaching tool. You will read a sentence aloud to the student and ask him to write it down without looking at a written model. Through this process, the student will learn to picture a grammatical, properly punctuated sentence in his head before setting it down on paper.*

To do dictation, explain to the student that he will write down the words that you are going to read, but that he will not be able to look at them. Read the selection aloud, slowly, once. Then say to the student, "Now I will read the sentence again, and then you will write it." Read it the second time and encourage the student to write without a further repetition. You are training the student not only to write correctly, but also to hear correctly. If he has not been used to doing this, it will take some practice on his part to listen actively. You should feel free to prompt him as necessary. By the end of second grade, the student should be able to hear a sentence once and write it.

Begin dictation with sentences of two or three words. The goal is to gradually lengthen the amount that the student is required to "hold in his mind" and then write down. Here are some helpful techniques for beginners:

> *Step 1. After you read a selection, ask the student to visualize the beginning capital letter and the end punctuation mark.*

> *Step 2. Repeat the sentence once more.*

> *Step 3. Have the student repeat what you just read.*

> *Step 4. Have him write what he just said if it is accurate. (If it is not accurate, repeat steps 1 & 2.)*

The first dictation exercise (below) is scripted for you; after this, dictation will appear at the end of lessons. Follow the same pattern given in the script. Be patient! Don't be surprised if the student appears to have forgotten all of his spelling and punctuation rules the first time he writes from dictation; this is a new skill and will take some time to master. Don't give up if the student complains; just shorten the amount done at one sitting, and keep practicing and gradually lengthening the amount included in one dictation. Most lessons will have a choice of options of length for dictations: 2–3 words, 5–6 words, or 7–10 words.

If you are teaching one student, watch the student as he writes. If he begins to make a mistake, stop him and have him correct the mistake immediately. If you are giving the dictation to more than one student, have the students make corrections at the end of the dictation by comparing it with the written model.

Instructor:　You have learned how to copy sentences. When you copy, you can look at the sentence and see that it begins with a capital letter. You can copy the punctuation mark at the end. You can copy the spelling of words and the spaces between them. Today, we are going to do something a little different. I am going to give you a sentence to write, but I am going to say it, rather than show it to you. I will say the sentence now. Listen very carefully to what I am about to read: "March is a windy month." What kind of letter does a sentence begin with?

Student: *A sentence begins with a capital letter.*

Instructor: What type of sentence is "March is a windy month"? Does it ask a question? Does it give a command? Does it show sudden, strong emotion? Does it give information?

Student: *The sentence gives information.*

Instructor: This sentence is a statement. What kind of punctuation mark goes at the end of a statement?

Student: *A statement ends with a period.*

Instructor: Now I will read the sentence to you one more time. Repeat it back to me: March is a windy month.

Student: *March is a windy month.*

Instructor: Now write that sentence on your own paper.

Note to Instructor: *Help the student sound out each word. Remind him as he writes to leave spaces between the words. Do not allow him to become frustrated with spelling—it is acceptable to tell him that the "e" sound at the end of "windy" is spelled with a "y." When he is finished writing from dictation, show him the original sentence in the book. Point out the capital letter, the period at the end, and the spacing between the words. Make corrections and praise him for doing a good job!*

10/23

••••••••••••••••••• **LESSON 23** ••••••••••••••••••

Introducing adjectives
Copywork: "June"

Note to Instructor: *The student will need art supplies or old magazines for summer pictures.*

Instructor: Repeat with me the definition of a noun.

TOGETHER: **A noun is the name of a person, place, thing, or idea.**

Instructor: A noun names, but it doesn't give any description of the person, place, or thing it names. If I say "flower" to you, you don't know whether it is blue or red, tall or tiny, wild, or in a pot. You can't make a picture of it in your mind. If I want to tell you more about the flower, I have to use other words to describe this naming word. I have to use **adjectives**. **An adjective is a word that describes a noun.** Let's say that together three times: **An adjective is a word that describes a noun.**

TOGETHER (three times): **An adjective is a word that describes a noun.**

Instructor: I am going to read to you some words that describe naming words. I want you to follow along as I read these adjectives—these describing words. When I say one of these adjectives, I want you to name a noun that it could describe!

Note to Instructor: *Show the following list to the student as you read. With your finger, point to each adjective as you read it. Then ask the student to name a person, place, or thing it could describe. (For example, point to "cold" and the student responds "ice." When you point and say "hot," the student might respond "chocolate.")*

cold, hot, round, square, sad, happy, funny, new, old, blue, red, tall, short, little, small, sticky, hungry, furry, white, curly, sour, sweet, tasty, crunchy, cloudy, soft, hard, fuzzy, huge, heavy, loud, seven, fifteen.

Instructor: Now, I want you to describe a noun. Think of every adjective that can possibly tell me more about this noun.

Note to Instructor: *Choose something in the room (a person or thing). Point to it. Help the student find adjectives to describe it. Ask him to tell you about its color, shape, and size. Encourage him to put his description into the form of a complete sentence, such as "The sofa is soft, green, and large."*

Instructor: Let's repeat the definition of an adjective together three more times. **An adjective is a word that describes a noun.**

TOGETHER (three times): **An adjective is a word that describes a noun.**

Copywork

Have the student copy the June couplet from the poem "The Year" (Lesson 11) onto a blank sheet of lined paper. If the student has great difficulty copying both lines of the couplet, have him copy one line and you write the second line. He can illustrate the paper by drawing a picture of a June activity (swimming, picnics, vacation, Flag Day, Father's Day). If he prefers, he can cut pictures from a magazine and paste them onto the page.

10/24

LESSON 24

Adjectives
Copywork: "July"

Note to Instructor: *The student will need art supplies or old magazines for summer pictures.*

The term "predicate adjective" is not taught until the next level of this program. In this level, the student will learn that adjectives are sometimes written next to the noun, but can also be written after a linking verb.

Instructor: We have learned that an **adjective** is a word that describes a noun. Let's repeat that definition together three times.

TOGETHER (three times): **An adjective is a word that describes a noun.**

Instructor: Today, let's practice using adjectives. First, let's think about words that describe how something tastes. What kind of adjectives tell us how a cookie tastes? How about a pickle? A potato chip? A piece of cake? An apple? A lemon? A taco?

Note to Instructor: *Encourage the student to use adjectives such as: sweet, sour, delicious, cold, warm, hot, spicy, juicy, etc.*

Instructor: Now let's think about adjectives that describe how something feels when you touch it. What if you were to touch the stove? How would it feel to touch an ice cube? How about a kitten? A patch of glue? Tree bark? Glass?

Note to Instructor: *Encourage the student to use adjectives such as: hot, cold, sticky, soft, hard, fuzzy, furry, rough, smooth, etc.*

Instructor: Sometimes adjectives come right next to the noun they describe. If I say "The happy baby giggled," what word describes "baby"?

Student: *"Happy" describes baby.*

Instructor: If I say "The baby is happy," does the word "happy" still describe the baby?

Student: *Yes, "happy" still describes the baby.*

Instructor: Sometimes adjectives come later in the sentence, after a linking verb. Do you remember your linking verbs? I will say them for you: "am, is, are, was, were, be, being, been." Let's say that together three times.

TOGETHER (three times): Am, is, are, was, were, be, being, been.

Instructor: If I say "I am hungry," can you find the linking verb in that sentence?

Note to Instructor: *Emphasize the word "am" slightly if the student is unable to identify the verb.*

Student: "Am" is the linking verb.

Instructor: In the sentence "I am hungry," which word describes me?
Student: Hungry.

Instructor: "Hungry" is an adjective. Now I would like you to write that sentence on your paper. Listen to me repeat it once more: "I am hungry." Repeat it back to me.
Student: I am hungry.

Instructor: Now write that sentence on your paper. Remember that the pronoun "I" is always capitalized!

Copywork

Read the July couplet from the poem "The Year" (Lesson 11) to the student. Point out the three adjectives in the couplet: "hot" describes "July," "stormy" describes "showers," and "lazy" describes "hours." Have the student copy the couplet onto a blank sheet of lined paper. If the student has great difficulty copying both lines, have him copy one line and you write the second line. He can illustrate the paper by drawing a picture of a July activity (swimming, Fourth of July, a beach trip). If he prefers, he can cut pictures from a magazine and paste them onto the page.

Enrichment Activity

Tell the student to use adjectives that describe the weather on a stormy day. After the student tells you as many as he can think of, give him these ideas: windy, cloudy, rainy, snowy, blustery, hot, warm, cold, cool, sunny. If you wish, he may write a short description of his stormy day and draw a picture showing his adjectives.

· **LESSON 25** ·

Nouns
Pronouns
Verbs
Adjectives
Copywork: "August"

Note to Instructor: *The student will need art supplies or old magazines for summer pictures.*

Instructor: We have learned about four different kinds of words: nouns, pronouns, verbs, and adjectives. Let's review what each kind of word does. **A noun is the name of a person, place, thing, or idea.** Let's repeat that together three times.

Together (three times): **A noun is the name of a person, place, thing, or idea.**

Instructor: Can you name a person for me? A place? A thing? An idea? All of those words are nouns.

Note to Instructor: *Give the student as much help as necessary to come up with these four nouns. You may have to remind him that an idea is something you think about in your mind, but cannot see or touch.*

Instructor: **A pronoun is a word used in the place of a noun.** Let's say that together three times.

Together (three times): **A pronoun is a word used in the place of a noun.**

Instructor: Instead of saying to you "Christina is coming to play today," I could say "She is coming to play today." Repeat those two sentences for me.
Student: *Christina is coming to play today. She is coming to play today.*

Instructor: The pronoun "she" is used in place of the noun "Christina." Now let's review our third kind of word: verbs. **A verb is a word that does an action, shows a state of being, links two words together, or helps another verb.** Let's say that together three times.

Together (three times): **A verb is a word that does an action, shows a state of being, links two words together, or helps another verb.**

Instructor: Can you finish these sentences for me, using action verbs? "The baby…"
Student: *The baby [laughed, drooled, crawled, giggled].*

Note to Instructor: *If necessary, prompt the student for the appropriate action verb.*

Instructor: The new puppy…

Student: *The new puppy [barked, played, slept].*

Instructor: These are verbs that do actions. Verbs also show state of being. The state of being verbs are: am, is, are, was, were, be, being, been. Let's repeat those together three times.

Together: (three times)
Am [clap]
Is [clap]
Are, was, were [clap]
Be [clap]
Being [clap]
Been [clap] [clap]

Instructor: Some verbs help other verbs. The helping verbs are: have, has, had, do, does, did, shall, will, should, would, may, might, must, can, could. Let's repeat those together three times.

TOGETHER: (three times)
Have, has, had [clap]
Do, does, did [clap]
Shall, will, should, would, may, might, must [clap] [clap]
Can, could!

Instructor: Sometimes a verb links two words together. If I say "You are smart!" I am using a pronoun in the place of a noun—your name. I am linking the pronoun "you" to a word that describes what you are—smart! The verb "are" links "you" with "smart." It is a **linking verb**. "Smart" is an adjective. It describes you! Let's review the definition of an adjective: **An adjective is a word that describes a noun**. Let's repeat that definition together three times.

TOGETHER (three times): **An adjective is a word that describes a noun.**

Instructor: I will give you some sentences with nouns and linking verbs. I want you to add an adjective to each sentence that describes the noun.

Note to Instructor: *If necessary, prompt the student to complete each sentence by asking questions such as "What color is the dress?" or "What size is the horse?"*

Instructor: The wall is…
Student: *The wall is [white].*

Instructor: The dress is…
Student: *The dress is [pretty, blue].*

Instructor: The horse is…

Student: *The horse is [big].*

Instructor: My room is…
Student: *My room is [neat, messy].*

Copywork

Look at the August couplet from "The Year" (Lesson 11) together. Help the student identify the nouns, verbs, and adjectives. See key below:

noun   action verb   adjective   noun
August brings the warmest air,

adjective noun   adjective   noun
Sandy feet and sea-wet hair.

Have the student copy the August couplet from the poem onto a blank sheet of lined paper. If the student has great difficulty copying both lines of the couplet, have him copy one line and you write the second line. He can illustrate the paper by drawing a picture of an August activity (eating ice cream, family birthdays, religious holidays). If he prefers, he can cut pictures from a magazine and paste them onto the page. (Note: the student should copy the couplet from page 23 in Lesson 11, not from the key above.)

• • • • • • • • • • • • • • • • •   **LESSON 26**   • • • • • • • • • • • • • • •

Helping verbs
Dictation exercise: "God has made them so"
Copywork: "September"

Notes to Instructor: *The student will need art supplies or old magazines for fall pictures.*

Review the helping verb chant today:

Am [clap]
Is [clap]
Are, was, were [clap]
Be [clap]
Being [clap]
Been [clap] [clap]
Have, has, had [clap]
Do, does, did [clap]
Shall, will, should, would, may, might, must [clap] [clap]
Can, could!

Instructor: Today I am going to give you some sentences in which the action verb needs another verb to help it. I will emphasize the verbs as I read. I want you to tell me which verb is the action verb, and which verb is the helping verb.

Note to Instructor: *Emphasize the italicized words in the following sentences. Give the student any necessary help. If the student cannot identify the helping verb, read the sentence without it and ask which word has disappeared.*

Instructor: "I'm glad the sky *is* painted blue." Which verb is the action verb? Which is the helping verb?
Student: *"Painted" is an action verb. "Is" is a helping verb.*

Instructor: "And the earth *is* painted green."
Student: *"Painted" is an action verb. "Is" is a helping verb.*

Instructor: Those sentences are the beginning of a poem. I am going to read the poem aloud while you follow along with me.

I'm glad the sky is painted blue,

And the earth is painted green,

With such a lot of nice fresh air

All sandwiched in between.

Instructor: Which helping verb do you see in line one?
Student: *Is.*

Instructor: Which helping verb do you see in line two?
Student: *Is.*

Instructor: This poem is an anonymous poem—we don't know who wrote it. Here is another line from a poem called "Against Quarrelling and Fighting." It was written by Isaac Watts.

Let dogs delight to bark and bite,

For God has made them so.

Instructor: The verbs in the last line are "has made." Which verb is the action verb? Which is the helping verb?
Student: *"Made" is an action verb. "Has" is a helping verb.*

Instructor: I will read you some more of the poem now:

Let dogs delight to bark and bite,

For God has made them so.

Let bears and lions growl and fight,

For it is their nature too.

But children, you should never let

Such angry passions rise;

Your little hands were never made

To tear each other's eyes.

Instructor: Listen to the verbs in this line: "But children, you should never let / Such angry passions rise." The verbs are "should" and "let." "Let" is the action verb. What is the helping verb?

Student: *"Should" is the helping verb.*

Instructor: "Should" helps the verb "let." Listen to this line: "Your little hands were never made / To tear each other's eyes."

Can you hear the verbs "were made"? "Were" is the helping verb. What is the action verb?

Student: *"Made" is the action verb.*

Dictation Exercise

Instructor: Now I would like you to write this sentence on your paper: "God has made them so." Listen to me as I say it again: "God has made them so." Can you repeat that sentence back to me?

Student: *God has made them so.*

Instructor: Write that sentence on your own paper. Remember that the first letter should be capitalized. What punctuation mark should come at the end of the sentence?

Student: *A period should come at the end of the sentence.*

Note to Instructor: *Repeat the dictation sentence once more, if necessary.*

Copywork

Have the student copy the September couplet from the poem "The Year" (Lesson 11) onto a blank sheet of lined paper. If the student has great difficulty copying both lines of the couplet, have him copy one line and you write the second line. He can illustrate the paper by drawing a picture of a September activity (fall leaves, books and pencils for "back to school," religious or family holidays). If he prefers, he can cut pictures from a magazine and paste them onto the page.

· **LESSON 27** ·

Story narration: "The Quarrel"

Note to Instructor: *Read aloud the old fable below and then ask the "starter questions" at the end of the story. Remember to encourage the student to answer in complete sentences. Then ask the student, "What is one thing you remember from the story?" Write his answer down and read it back to him.*

The Quarrel
An old fable

Once upon a time, all of the different parts of the body started to quarrel with each other. "We do all of the work around here!" the legs complained. "We take the rest of you where you need to go. Our muscles work and work—and the rest of you don't do anything to help us out."

"You think you work hard?" groaned the feet. "What about us? We carry everyone else's weight! And we're stuck in these hot, dark shoes all day long. We can't even see where we're going! We work much harder than the legs!"

The hands snapped, "Stop whining. If we didn't open doors, you'd be stuck in one place. We do all of the work—carrying toys, holding pencils for writing, patting dirty dogs. And we're always being washed with nasty soap! Even when the feet and legs are relaxing, we're still at work—feeding the mouth, or turning pages of books. We have the most difficult time of all."

"What are you complaining about?" asked the mouth. "You may put the food into me—but I have to chew it! I chew and chew, and chew—and you're not even grateful! You get all the nutrition from the food I swallow. I'm not going to feed you any more!"

"You're all wrong," grumbled the eyes. "We work all day long. We're open from dawn to dusk. We have to keep on watching even when the rest of you are doing nothing. If we weren't looking out for you, the legs and feet would be running into walls all of the time, and the hands wouldn't be able to find toys or food. What ingratitude! We're not going to look out for you any more."

"Fine!" said the legs. "We quit!"

"So do we!" squeaked the feet. "No more walking!"

The legs, the feet, the hands, the eyes, and the mouth all sulked. They refused to do anything. The body didn't get fed. It didn't get any exercise. It couldn't even watch TV! It got thinner and weaker and more and more bored.

Finally the parts of the body held a meeting. "I haven't eaten for days," the mouth groaned. "I've almost forgotten how."

"We have nothing to do!" moaned the hands.

"We are weak and helpless without food and exercise!" agreed the legs and the feet.

"Let's all agree to work together," suggested the eyes. "None of us can work unless the others do their jobs. Instead of complaining about who does the most, let's each do our own tasks. We'll go back to looking out for the rest of you. The legs and feet can carry us around. The mouth can feed us, and the hands can work for us. Then the body will be healthy again."

So the parts of the body agreed to help each other, rather than quarrelling about who worked the hardest. Soon the body was strong and healthy again—and the legs, feet, hands, mouth, and eyes were happy once more.

Note to Instructor: *Use these questions to help the student summarize the story.*

Instructor: Why did the legs complain?
Student: *The legs said that they worked harder than anyone else.*

Instructor: What did the ~~shoes~~ feet complain about?
Student: *They were stuck in hot shoes and worked harder than the legs.*

Instructor: What sorts of things did the hands do for the body?
Student: *The hands carried toys, held pencils, patted dogs, fed the mouth, turned pages of books.*

Instructor: What did the parts of the body decide to do?
Student: *Each part decided to refuse to do its work.*

Instructor: What happened to the body?
Student: *It got weak, thin, and bored.*

Instructor: What did the parts of the body decide to do then?
Student: *They decided to help each other again.*

10/30

· · · · · · · · · · · · · · · · · · ·   **LESSON 28**   · · · · · · · · · · · · · · · ·

Contractions
Copywork: "October"
Poem review: "The Goops" (Lesson 2)

Note to Instructor: *The student will need art supplies or October pictures to cut and paste.*

Review "The Goops" today.

Instructor: We have learned that **a contraction is made up of two words, put together into one word, with some letters left out.** A punctuation mark called an apostrophe is put in the place of the missing letters. Let's read back through "The Quarrel" together and find all of the contractions. When we find each contraction, we will decide for which two words it stands. I will write those words out for you next to each contraction.

Note to Instructor: *As you find each contraction, write it on your paper. Across from it, write the full form of the word. Use the key below:*

Paragraph 1:	don't	do not
Paragraph 2:	we're	we are
	can't	can not
	we're	we are
Paragraph 3:	didn't	did not
	you'd	you would
	we're	we are
	we're	we are
Paragraph 4:	you're	you are
	I'm	I am
Paragraph 5:	You're	You are
	we're	we are
	weren't	were not
	wouldn't	would not
	we're	we are
Paragraph 6:	none	
Paragraph 7:	none	
Paragraph 8:	didn't	did not
	didn't	did not
	couldn't	could not
Paragraph 9:	haven't	have not
	I've	I have
Paragraph 10:	none	
Paragraph 11:	none	

Paragraph 12:	Let's	Let us
	let's	let us
	We'll	We will
Paragraph 13:	none	

Copywork

Have the student copy the October couplet from the poem "The Year" (Lesson 11) onto a blank sheet of lined paper. If the student has great difficulty copying both lines of the couplet, have him copy one line and you write the second line. He can illustrate the paper by drawing a picture of an October activity (frost, pumpkins, fall leaves, holidays). If he prefers, he can cut pictures from a magazine and paste them onto the page.

·················· **LESSON 29** ··················

Four kinds of verbs review
Copywork: "November"

Note to Instructor: *The student will need art supplies or November pictures to cut and paste.*

Instructor: **A verb is a word that does an action, shows a state of being, links two words together, or helps another verb.** Let's say the definition of a verb together.

Together: **A verb is a word that does an action, shows a state of being, links two words together, or helps another verb.**

Instructor: This tells us that there are four kinds of verbs: action verbs, state of being verbs, linking verbs, and helping verbs. Action verbs tell about something you can do. I will say some action verbs, and I want you to act them out: wiggle, hop, crawl, stand, smile, giggle. Now I want you to stand perfectly still and just be. State of being verbs tell us that something exists. The state of being verbs are: Am, is, are, was, were, be, being, been. Let's repeat those together.

Together: Am [clap]
Is [clap]
Are, was, were [clap]
Be [clap]
Being [clap]
Been [clap] [clap]

Instructor: Some verbs help other verbs. The helping verbs are the verbs we just said as well as: Have, has, had, do, does, did, shall, will, should, would, may, might, must, can, could. Let's repeat those additional helping verbs together.

Together: Have, has, had [clap]
Do, does, did [clap]
Shall, will, should, would, may, might, must [clap] [clap]
Can, could!

Instructor: Linking verbs connect two words together. If I say "The mouth was upset, and the eyes were annoyed," I am linking "mouth" with "upset" by using the linking verb "was." I am linking "eyes" with "annoyed" by using the linking verb "were." Now we are going to look at a poem together. This poem has both action verbs and helping verbs in it. We will try to find all of the action verbs and all of the helping verbs. First I will read the poem "How Creatures Move," and then we will look for helping verbs and action verbs.

Note to Instructor: *Read the poem all the way through as the student listens. Then, read the poem again. Use your finger to help the student follow along as you read, stopping as necessary to identify the helping verbs and action verbs. The helping verbs and action verbs are as follows:*

walks (action), leaps (action), can (helping), crawl (action), can (helping), dive (action), swim (action), wiggles (action), swings (action), may (helping), hop (action), spread (action), sail (action), have (this is an action verb, but since "have" can be used in both ways, don't correct him if he names it as a helping verb), leap (action), dance (action), walk (action), run (action).

How Creatures Move
Anonymous

The lion walks on padded paws,

The squirrel leaps from limb to limb,

While flies can crawl straight up a wall,

And seals can dive and swim.

The worm, he wiggles all around,

The monkey swings by his tail,

And birds may hop upon the ground,

Or spread their wings and sail.

But boys and girls have much more fun;

They leap and dance

And walk and run.

Copywork

Have the student copy the November couplet from the poem "The Year" (Lesson 11) onto a blank sheet of lined paper. If the student has great difficulty copying both lines of the couplet, have him copy one line and you write the second line. He can illustrate the paper by drawing a picture of a November activity (religious holidays, Thanksgiving). If he prefers, he can paste pictures onto the page.

••••••••••••••••••••• **LESSON 30** •••••••••••••••••••

Adjectives
Copywork: "December"

Note to Instructor: *The student will need art supplies or December pictures to cut and paste.*

Instructor: In the poem "How Creatures Move," the lion "walks on padded paws." "Padded" is a word that describes "paws." It tells you more about the paws. "Padded" is an adjective that describes the noun "paws." **An adjective is a word that describes a noun.** Let's repeat that definition together three times.

Together (three times): **An adjective is a word that describes a noun.**

Instructor: Let's practice making up some sentences that use adjectives. I will suggest the names of people, places, and things. You will tell me some adjectives that describe them, and I will write those adjectives down. Then I will help you to put your adjectives into complete sentences.

Note to Instructor: *List the names of three people, places, or things that the student can look at—either in the room or in a magazine or book. It is important for the student to have an actual, concrete image to describe. Write the adjectives down as the student says them. You can help the student by prompting him with these questions: "What color is it? What size is it? Is it young or old? How many? How does it feel? How does it smell? How does it taste? What shape is it?" After you have written down a list of adjectives for each noun, help the student form the description into a complete sentence, such as: "The little brown dog is fluffy and cute," or "The chair is big, blue, and soft." Choose one of these sentences and repeat it back to the student several times. Then ask the student to write the sentence from dictation. If the sentence has more than two adjectives in a row (for example, "My book is thick, brown, and square"), you may need to review commas in a series (Lesson 14).*

Copywork

Have the student copy the December couplet from the poem "The Year" (Lesson 11) onto a blank sheet of lined paper. If the student has great difficulty copying both lines of the couplet, have him copy one line and you write the second line. He can illustrate the paper by drawing a picture of a December activity (snow, ice, religious holidays). If he prefers, he can paste pictures onto the page.

• • • • • • • • • • • • • • • • LESSON 31 • • • • • • • • • • • • • • •

Poem memorization: "The Year"

Note to Instructor: *Read this poem out loud three times. Later in the day, read it again three times. See Lesson 2 for memorization techniques.*

The Year

By Sara Coleridge, adapted by Sara Buffington

January brings the snow,
Helps the skis and sleds to go.

February brings the rain,
Thaws the frozen lake again.

March brings breezes loud and shrill,
Stirs the dancing daffodil.

April brings the primrose sweet,
Scatters daisies at our feet.

May brings sunshine full and bright,
Sends the busy bees to flight.

June brings tulips, lilies, roses,
Fills the children's hands with posies.

Hot July brings stormy showers,
Lemonade, and lazy hours.

August brings the warmest air,
Sandy feet and sea-wet hair.

September brings the fruit so sweet,
Apples ripe from summer heat.

October brings the colored trees,
Scampering squirrels and cooling breeze.

Dull November brings the blast,
Then the leaves are whirling fast.

Chill December brings the sleet,
Blazing fire, and Christmas treat.[1]

1 Alternate last line: "Blazing fire, and winter treat."

••••••••••••••••••••• **LESSON 32** •••••••••••••••••••

Introducing interjections
Four types of sentences
Copywork: "Ouch!"
Poem review: "The Year" (Lesson 31)

Note to Instructor: *Read the poem "The Year" out loud three times.*

Instructor: A few lessons ago (Lesson 27), we read a story about a quarrel between the parts of the body. The story was interesting to read because it contained so many different types of sentences. It didn't just state facts. Sometimes the parts of the body made statements, sometimes they gave commands, sometimes they asked questions, and sometimes they used exclamations! We are going to read some of those sentences again today. But first we are going to review the definition of a sentence. **A sentence is a group of words that expresses a complete thought.** Let's say that definition together three times.

TOGETHER (three times): **A sentence is a group of words that expresses a complete thought.**

Instructor: **A sentence begins with a capital letter and ends with a punctuation mark.** Let's say that together three times.

TOGETHER (three times): **A sentence begins with a capital letter and ends with a punctuation mark.**

Instructor: Remember the four different types of sentences? They are statements, commands, questions, and exclamations. Repeat with me three times: statements, commands, questions, and exclamations.

TOGETHER (three times): Statements, commands, questions, and exclamations.

Instructor: **A statement gives information.** Repeat that definition for me: **A statement gives information.**

Student: *A statement gives information.*

Instructor: Here is a statement from the story "The Quarrel": "Once upon a time, all of the different parts of the body started to quarrel with each other." Here is another statement: "The legs, the feet, the hands, the eyes, and the mouth all sulked." Both of those sentences give you information. They are statements. They end with a period. The second type of sentence is a command. **A command gives an order or makes a request.** Let's say that together twice: **A command gives an order or makes a request.**

TOGETHER (twice): **A command gives an order or makes a request.**

Instructor: In the story, when the hands became irritated because the feet and legs were complaining, the hands snapped, "Stop whining." The hands gave an order or made a request that the feet and legs stop whining. "Stop whining" is a command. The third type of sentence is a question. **A question asks something. It ends with a question mark.** Let's say the definition of a question together three times: **A question asks something. It ends with a question mark.**

TOGETHER (three times): **A question asks something. It ends with a question mark.**

Instructor: In the story, the feet asked the legs, "You think you work hard?" "What about us?" Those are questions. The feet asked the legs for information! The fourth type of sentence is an exclamation. **An exclamation shows sudden or strong feeling. It ends with an exclamation point.** Say that with me three times: **An exclamation shows sudden or strong feeling. It ends with an exclamation point.**

TOGETHER (three times): **An exclamation shows sudden or strong feeling. It ends with an exclamation point.**

Instructor: The story of the quarrel was full of sudden and strong feelings. The parts of the body were showing lots of strong feelings when they were quarrelling. Do you ever quarrel or fuss with anyone? Do you have sudden and strong feelings when you quarrel and fuss? But there are other times when we show sudden or strong feelings, but we aren't quarrelling. Other sudden or strong feelings can be excitement: "We're going to see a baby panda!" Or surprise: "Thank you for this present!" Or happiness: "Spring always makes me feel happy!" You might have a sudden or strong feeling of fear and concern if you think someone is going to get hurt. At a time like that, you might yell "That's hot!" because the baby is about to touch a hot stove.

We have learned about the ways that different kinds of words work together in these sentences. We have learned about nouns, pronouns, verbs, and adjectives. **A noun is the name of a person, place, thing, or idea. A pronoun is a word used in the place of a noun. A verb is a word that does an action, shows a state of being, links two words together, or helps another verb. An adjective is a word that describes a noun.** Today we are going to talk about another kind of word called an **interjection**. When we say just one word suddenly with sudden or strong feeling, we call that word an interjection. Interjections are followed by exclamation points. Say the definition of an interjection with me three times: **An interjection is a word that expresses sudden or strong feeling.**

TOGETHER (three times): **An interjection is a word that expresses sudden or strong feeling.**

Instructor: I am going to tell you something imaginary that happened, and I want you to tell me a word that you might say. That word is an interjection! Running across the yard, you stepped on something sharp and cut your foot. What would you have said?

Student: *[Ouch!]*

Instructor: ["Ouch"] is an interjection. Now imagine that your baby sister is about to run into the street. What would you say?

Student: [Stop!]

Instructor: ["Stop"] is an interjection. Now imagine that you're at the grocery store. You are walking slo-o-wly! But your mother wants to move fast and finish the shopping. What word might your mother interject into her conversation to get you to speed up?

Student: [Hurry!]

Instructor: ["Hurry"] is an interjection. When we write an interjection, we put an exclamation point after the interjection. When an interjection is all alone with an exclamation point after it, it should begin with a capital letter.

Copywork

Have the student copy one of these sentences of appropriate length for his ability. Remind him that the interjection begins with a capital letter and ends with an exclamation point. If necessary, remind him that the sentence following the exclamation begins with a capital letter and ends with a period.

Ouch! I just cut my foot.

Stop! Don't run into the street.

Hurry! If we don't finish shopping, we won't get home on time.

11/13

Adjectives
Commas in a series
Dictation exercise: "The brown bird"
Poem review: "The Year" (Lesson 31)

Note to Instructor: *Review "The Year" today.*

Instructor:	Last lesson, we learned about **interjections. An interjection is a word that expresses sudden or strong feeling.** Let's repeat that together three times.
TOGETHER:	**An interjection is a word that expresses sudden or strong feeling.**
Instructor:	Let's imagine that I walked into a room, saw something sitting on a table, and said, "Wow!" That's an interjection. Then I added three more interjections: "Fantastic! Delicious! Yummy!" What do you think that I just saw?
Student:	*You saw something to eat!*
Instructor:	Let's think about words that describe delicious, yummy, fantastic foods. Let's start with cake. The word "cake" is a noun, because cake is a thing. Do you remember what words describe nouns?
Student:	*An adjective is a word that describes a noun.*
Instructor:	Any words that you use to describe the noun "cake" will be adjectives. Let's think of some adjectives that describe "cake," and I will write them down.

Note to Instructor: *If necessary, prompt the student with the following list: chocolate, strawberry, vanilla, caramel, lemon, layer, round, square, birthday, gooey, delicious, scrumptious, frosted, glazed, decorated. Write down adjectives as the student gives them.*

Instructor:	Now put four of those adjectives into a sentence that begins "The cake was…" Say that sentence to me, and I will write it down.
Student:	*The cake was [chocolate, round, frosted, and gooey].*

Note to Instructor: *Write the sentence down for the student. Put a comma after each item in the list; use the word "and" before the last item, as illustrated above. Point to each comma.*

Instructor:	Look at this sentence with me. What punctuation mark separates the adjectives in the list?
Student:	*A comma separates the adjectives.*

Instructor: Words in a list should be separated by commas. We could put an "and" between each one of these adjectives: The cake was [chocolate and round and frosted and gooey]. But that would sound awkward. So we just put a comma between each adjective instead. Let's make another "food list." Tell me a food that you enjoy, and then we will think of adjectives to describe it.

Note to Instructor: *Help the student think of a food noun and of at least four adjectives that describe it. Ask the student to put the noun and adjectives into a sentence following the format above: "The [food] is [adjective], [adjective], [adjective], and [adjective]." Write the sentence down. Remind the student that these describing words are adjectives. Point to each comma, and then remind the student that words in a list should be separated by commas.*

Dictation Exercise

Choose an appropriate sentence from the list below and dictate to the student. Repeat the sentence twice and then ask the student to repeat it back to you before he begins to write. Remind him that commas follow items in a list. Tell him that when you are reading aloud, you will pause whenever a comma comes in the sentence; as you read, pause for a few moments at each comma. Remember to watch the student and correct any mistakes as he writes.

The bird was brown.

The robin hops, sings, and pecks.

The robin pulls, tugs, and eats worms from the ground.

11/14

Parts of Speech
Introducing conjunctions
Dictation exercise: "I was tired"
Poem review: "The Year" (Lesson 31)

Note to Instructor: *Review "The Year" today.*

Instructor: In a car, all the parts of the motor have to do their jobs properly to make a car run. All the parts of a washing machine have to work together properly to make a washing machine work. Have you wondered why we are learning about these nouns, pronouns, verbs, adjectives, and interjections? It is because they are called "parts of speech." The parts of speech make a sentence work properly—just like the parts of a motor make a car work properly. If you wanted to build a car motor, you would need to know all of the different parts. And if you want to make a good sentence, you need to know all of the sentence parts! So far, we have learned about nouns, pronouns, verbs, adjectives, and interjections. I am going to review them with you. After I tell you what the part of speech does in a sentence, repeat the definition with me.

Instructor: **A noun is the name of a person, place, thing, or idea.**

Together: **A noun is the name of a person, place, thing, or idea.**

Instructor: **A pronoun is a word used in the place of a noun.**

Together: **A pronoun is a word used in the place of a noun.**

Instructor: **A verb is a word that does an action, shows a state of being, links two words together, or helps another verb.**

Together: **A verb is a word that does an action, shows a state of being, links two words together, or helps another verb.**

Instructor: **An adjective is a word that describes a noun.**

Together: **An adjective is a word that describes a noun.**

Instructor: **An interjection is a word that expresses sudden or strong feeling.**

Together: **An interjection is a word that expresses sudden or strong feeling.**

Instructor: Now we are going to learn about another little part of speech. It is called a **conjunction**. Sometimes, when you are in the car on the highway, you might see a sign that says "Junction." A "junction" sign means that two roads are joining together. "Junction" means "joining." A conjunction is a word that joins words or groups of words together. I am going to say the definition of a conjunction for you slowly, then you join with me as we say it three times more. **A conjunction joins words or groups of words together**.

TOGETHER (three times): **A conjunction joins words or groups of words together**.

Instructor: The conjunctions you will use most often are "and," "but," "or." If you were going to tell me that two kinds of pets—rabbits and hamsters—both eat lettuce, you would say, "Rabbits and hamsters eat lettuce." The conjunction "and" joins the words "rabbits" and "hamsters." Can you tell me a sentence about two things that can fly?

Student: *[Birds and butterflies] fly.*

Instructor: Now, tell me a sentence about two things that can swim.

Student: *[Fish and tadpoles] swim.*

Instructor: In both of these sentences you used "and" to join the names of two things. Now, let's make some sentences that use "and" to join two action words. I can walk and write. The dog barks and chases. Now tell me two actions you can do.

Student: *[I can run and jump.]*

Instructor: The conjunction "and" usually connects two words together. The conjunction "or" usually means that you will have to choose between the two words that are joined! If I say "Play a game or go to bed," the conjunction "or" joins together two actions—but you can't do both. You will have to choose one or the other! If I say "You can wear your blue sweater or your red sweatshirt," you can pick one or the other—but you can't wear both! Think about two things that I could do. Now, make a sentence that gives me permission to do one thing or the other.

Student: *[You can go swimming or you can use the computer.]*

Instructor: The last conjunction is "but." If I say "I started to read my book, but I fell asleep," I am joining together two groups of words. "I started to read my book" is joined to "I fell asleep." Now I will give you two groups of words. I want you to join them together with the conjunction "but." "I want to go outside." "I cannot find my coat." Join those together with the conjunction "but."

Student: *I want to go outside, but I cannot find my coat.*

Instructor: Let's repeat that definition three more times: **A conjunction joins words or groups of words together**.

TOGETHER (three times): **A conjunction joins words or groups of words together**.

Dictation Exercise

Choose one or more of the following sentences. Remind the student that you will pause wherever a comma should go.

I was tired, and I slept.

I want to go outside, but I can't find my coat.

You can go swimming, or you can use the computer.

• • • • • • • • • • • • • • • • •   **LESSON 35**   • • • • • • • • • • • • • • • •

Interjections
Conjunctions
Dictation exercise: "The zoo"
Poem review: "The Goops" (Lesson 2)

Note to Instructor: *Review "The Goops" today.*

The student may need art supplies for the enrichment activity.

Instructor: Let's review some of the definitions we've learned. Repeat this with me three times: **An interjection is a word that expresses sudden or strong feeling.**

TOGETHER (three times): **An interjection is a word that expresses sudden or strong feeling.**

Instructor (with feeling!): Oh! Fantastic! Wonderful! Great!

Note to Instructor: *Pause for a moment to see whether the student recognizes your use of interjections. If not, point out that you have just expressed strong feeling with the words above.*

Instructor: If I say "Wonderful! You are using your brain and getting your work done," I am joining together two groups of words. I am joining "You are using your brain" to "getting your work done" with the conjunction "and." Remember: **A conjunction joins words or groups of words together.** Let's repeat that together three times.

TOGETHER (three times): **A conjunction joins words or groups of words together.**

Instructor: The conjunctions you will use most often are: "and," "but," "or." Say these sentences after me: "I would eat my spinach, but I am not hungry."
Student: *I would eat my spinach, but I am not hungry.*

Instructor: "You may eat your spinach, or you may choose Brussels sprouts instead."
Student: *You may eat your spinach, or you may choose Brussels sprouts instead.*

Instructor: Both sentences used a conjunction to join groups of words. What conjunction does the first sentence use? Listen to it again: "I would eat my spinach, but I am not hungry."
Student: *The sentence uses the conjunction "but."*

Instructor: What conjunction does the second sentence use? Listen to it again: "You may eat your spinach, or you may choose Brussels sprouts instead."
Student: *The sentence uses the conjunction "or."*

Instructor: Now I will use the conjunction "and" to join words together. "I went to the zoo and saw a monkey and a lion and a zebra and a giraffe." I will write that sentence down for you.

Note to Instructor: *Write the above sentence on your paper.*

Instructor: In Lesson 14 we talked about using commas to separate items in a series—a list of items. When you have more than two items in your list, you use commas instead of conjunctions. I will write this sentence again, using commas to separate the list of animals that you saw at the zoo. "I went to the zoo and saw a monkey, a lion, a zebra, and a giraffe."

Note to Instructor: *Write the above sentence on your paper. Point out the commas. Remind the student that the last "and" should remain in the list.*

Instructor: Items in a series should be separated by commas. Items in a series can be nouns—like the names of the animals. Commas are also used in sentences to separate adjectives that describe things. If I write "The zoo is hot and interesting and noisy and crowded," I am listing adjectives that describe the zoo. I am joining those adjectives with the conjunction "and."

Note to Instructor: *Write the sentence above on your paper. Point out the adjectives and the conjunctions.*

Instructor: But it would be easier to use commas to separate those adjectives. Now I will write "The zoo is hot, interesting, noisy, and crowded." Commas will replace all of the "and"s— except for the very last one.

Note to Instructor: *Write the above sentence on your paper. Point out the commas. Remind the student that the last "and" should remain in the list.*

Instructor: If I write "I walked and laughed and pointed and saw animals at the zoo," I am listing four actions that you can do. Those actions are also items in a series. I am joining them together with the conjunction "and."

Note to Instructor: *Write the sentence above on your paper. Point out the adjectives and the conjunctions.*

Instructor: It would be better to use commas to separate those actions. I will write "I walked, laughed, pointed, and saw animals at the zoo." Now commas separate those items in a series.

Note to Instructor: *Write the above sentence on your paper. Point out the commas. Remind the student that the last "and" should remain in the list.*

Dictation Exercise

Choose one or more of the following sentences. Remind the student that you will pause wherever a comma should go. Remember to pause at each comma!

The baby is sweet, fat, and damp.

The zoo is hot, interesting, noisy, and crowded.

The legs, the feet, the hands, the eyes, and the mouth all sulked.

Enrichment Activity

Help the student make up sentences that have items in a list. Ask the student for a series of adjectives that describe a favorite activity, a list of activities that he enjoys, and a list of things in his room. Help him to write the sentences out, using commas properly. He may illustrate the lists. Title the paper "Items in a Series."

11/20

····················· **LESSON 36** ···················

Introducing letter-writing: Writing a thank-you note
Poem review: "The Year" (Lesson 31)

Notes to Instructor: *Review "The Year" today.*

Today you will begin to help the student write a thank-you note to an adult using a title of respect. Even if the adult is a close relative, practice using a title of respect. Using the form below as a model for a friendly letter, you will write for the student a rough draft of a real thank-you note to a real person, thanking them for a real gift. Use the suggestions in the model to help the student compose the letter's content. Then, write your rough draft in proper form, so that the student can copy directly from it.

You will address an envelope and mail the letter in the next lesson. If the student mails this note to a relative, you should put a note in the envelope explaining that the student is practicing writing titles of respect.

> **Date** (Today's date, written on the right-hand side of the paper)

Greeting (Dear _____,)
(Remember that a comma comes after the greeting. Remind the student that a title of respect which is abbreviated begins with a capital letter and has a period following it).

Body of the Letter (Thank you for the _____. Here, name the gift. Help the student tell something he liked about the gift, choosing an appropriate adjective to describe it [pretty, big, little, cute, special, bright, good, delicious, funny, interesting]. Then ask him to describe how he will use the gift. If he is writing a thank-you note for a trip or for some other favor, have him describe his favorite part of the trip or favor. The body of the letter should be one brief paragraph. Remember to indent the first line of this paragraph.)

> **Closing** (You may use "Love," "Sincerely," or "Yours truly." Remember that a comma comes after the closing. The closing should be in line with the date above.)
>
> **Writer's Name** (Student signs his own name.)

Note to Instructor: *Now ask the student to copy the letter neatly onto his own paper. Supervise as the student copies the letter, reminding him of needed corrections as necessary. If the student is frustrated by the length of the copywork, you may finish the letter for him. In the next lesson he will address an envelope and mail the letter.*

11/21

••••••••••••••••••••• **LESSON 37** ••••••••••••••••••••

Addressing an envelope

Note to Instructor: *Both you and the student will need a business-size envelope. The student will also need a first-class stamp.*

Today the student will address a real envelope for the thank-you note he wrote last lesson. (Using a business-size envelope will give a young student more room to write!) You will address a model envelope for him. Write his name and address on the top left-hand corner of the envelope. As you are writing, remind him to abbreviate street names properly, to capitalize names of cities, etc., to use the proper postal code for his state, and to use his ZIP code. Write the recipient's name and address in the center of the envelope. As you are writing, remind the student to use a period after titles of respect and other appropriate abbreviations. After you finish writing the model envelope, draw light lines on a second envelope as below:

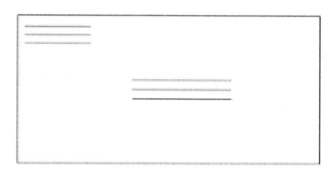

Most young students need lines to guide them as they write. Help the student to copy the names and addresses onto his own envelope, to fold the letter neatly and put it in the envelope, and to mail it. Remember that letters should be folded into thirds: first, fold up the bottom third, and then fold down the top third.

Remind the student to "write small"! If he becomes frustrated, you may finish writing the address for him so that he can stamp and mail the letter.

11/21

· **LESSON 38** ·

Introducing direct quotations
Quotation marks
Copywork: "The Little Bird"

Note to Instructor: *Chant the helping verb list three times with the student:*
Am [clap]
Is [clap]
Are, was, were [clap]
Be [clap]
Being [clap]
Been [clap] [clap]
Have, has, had [clap]
Do, does, did [clap]
Shall, will, should, would, may, might, must [clap] [clap]
Can, could!

Instructor: I am going to read a poem called "The Little Bird" to you. Listen as I read.

Note to Instructor: *Read the following poem without showing it to the student. Make a distinct voice for the quotation (the bold print).*

The Little Bird
Mother Goose rhyme

Once I saw a little bird

Come hop, hop, hop;

So I cried, "**Little bird,**

Will you stop, stop, stop?"

And was going to the window

To say "**How do you do?**"

But he shook his little tail,

And far away he flew.

Instructor: Now I will show you the poem and read it again. Follow along with your eyes as I read. This time, I want you to read the words that the child says in the poem.

Note to Instructor: *Read the poem again, running your finger under the words you are saying as the student follows along. When you get to the direct quotations, pause and let the student read the bold print.*

Instructor: The words that you read are called **direct quotations. Direct quotations** are the exact words that someone says. Look back at the exact words that the child says in the poem when she sees the bird. There are special punctuation marks on either side of those exact words. We call these **quotation marks. Quotation marks** are two apostrophes, put together. You learned how to make apostrophes when we learned about contractions (Lesson 19).

Note to Instructor: *Write out the contraction "can't" on your paper, and show the student the apostrophe.*

Instructor: Now, I will make quotation marks for you on my paper, and then you will practice making quotation marks as well.

Note to Instructor: *Make several sets of quotation marks for the student to copy. Consult your handwriting program for the style of quotation marks.*

Copywork

Choose one or more of the sentences below for the student to copy.

"How do you do?"

"Little bird, will you stop, stop, stop?"

So I cried, "Little bird, will you stop, stop, stop?"

• • • • • • • • • • • • • • • • • • **LESSON 39** • • • • • • • • • • • • • • • • •

Poem memorization: "The Little Bird"

Note to Instructor: *Read this poem out loud three times. Later in the day, read it again three times. See Lesson 2 for memorization techniques. Because this is such a short poem, the student may be able to memorize it in a brief time. Encourage him to use a special voice for the quotations in the poem.*

The Little Bird
Mother Goose rhyme

Once I saw a little bird
Come hop, hop, hop;
So I cried, "Little bird,
Will you stop, stop, stop?"
And was going to the window
To say "How do you do?"
But he shook his little tail,
And far away he flew.

12|6|19

••••••••••••••••••• **LESSON 40** •••••••••••••••••••

Story narration: "The Little Red Hen"
Copywork: "The Little Red Hen"
Poem review: "The Little Bird" (Lesson 39)

Notes to Instructor: *In Lesson 49, the student will need five or six first-class postcard stamps and postcards to address to relatives. Plan now to have these on hand.*

Review "The Little Bird" today.

Read aloud the folk tale below. Then ask the "starter questions" at the end of the story. Remember to encourage the student to answer in complete sentences. Then ask the student, "What is one thing you remember from the story?" Write his answer down and read it back to him.

The Little Red Hen
A folk tale

The Little Red Hen was walking along the road with the dog, the cat, and the duck when she found some wheat that had been dropped by a farmer when he harvested his field.

"Who will help me plant this wheat?" said the Little Red Hen.

"Not I," said the dog.

"Not I," said the cat.

"Not I," said the duck.

"Then I will plant the wheat," said the Little Red Hen.

So the Little Red Hen called her little chicks to help her. Together, they scratched out a little place in the garden and planted the wheat.

A rain shower watered the wheat seeds, and the sun warmed the soil. By and by, tiny green shoots of wheat began to come up. But grass seeds and weed seeds, sown by the wind, also began to come up. The weeds began to crowd out the tiny little wheat shoots.

"Who will help pull the grass and weeds out of the garden of wheat?" said the Little Red Hen.

"Not I," said the dog.

"Not I," said the cat.

"Not I," said the duck.

"Then my chicks and I will keep the grass and weeds from crowding out the tiny, little wheat plants," said the Little Red Hen. She called her chicks, and they ran happily to help her. They tended the little garden of wheat for many weeks, pulling weeds and grass. Often she asked, "Who will help pull the grass and weeds out of the garden of wheat?" But the cat, the dog, and the duck lay outside the garden, resting and watching while the hen and her chicks worked.

The wheat grew tall, and soon was ready to harvest. "Who will help me harvest the wheat?" said the Little Red Hen.

"Not I," said the dog.

"Not I," said the cat.

"Not I," said the duck.

"Then my chicks and I will harvest it," said the Little Red Hen. She cut down the stalks of wheat with her sharp bill, so that they lay on the ground. Then she called her chicks. "Now we must take the wheat to the thresher," she said, "so that he can separate the grains of wheat from the stalks! Who will help us carry the wheat down the road to the thresher?"

"Not I," said the dog.

"Not I," said the cat.

"Not I," said the duck.

"Then we will do it alone," said the Little Red Hen. Her little chicks ran back and forth, helping her take the wheat to the thresher, one stalk at a time. He separated the wheat from the stalks, so that the hen and her chicks had a big bag of grain.

"Who will help me take the bag of wheat to the miller, so that he can grind it into flour?" said the Little Red Hen.

"Not I," said the dog.

"Not I," said the cat.

"Not I," said the duck.

"Then we will," said the Little Red Hen. So she and the chicks dragged the bag of wheat all the way to the miller. After the miller ground the wheat into a fine flour, the Little Red Hen said, "Who will help me bake some bread?"

"Not I," said the dog.

"Not I," said the cat.

"Not I," said the duck.

"Then we will bake the bread," said the Little Red Hen and her chicks. Her little chicks loved to help their mother in the kitchen. They mixed and kneaded and shaped the bread into loaves and let it rise. Then they stoked the fire and put the bread into the oven to bake. The smell of the bread floated out into the yard. The dog, the cat, and the duck smelled the bread. They wandered lazily over to the kitchen. There, they found the Little Red Hen, just taking the warm fragrant bread out of the oven. The little chicks all crowded around, ready to eat.

"Who will eat this loaf?" asked the Little Red Hen.

"I will!" said the dog.

"I will!" said the cat.

"I will!" said the duck.

"No, you won't!" said the Little Red Hen. "You would not help plant the grain, nor weed the garden, nor take the wheat to the thresher and miller. You would not help make the bread. So now you will not eat any bread! My chicks and I will eat it together."

So the Little Red Hen together with her helpful chicks enjoyed their delicious warm bread, fresh from the oven.

Instructor: What did the Little Red Hen find that had been dropped by the farmer?
Student: *The Little Red Hen found some wheat.*

Instructor: Who would not help her plant the wheat?
Student: *The dog, cat, and duck would not help.*

Instructor: After the hen planted her wheat, what else grew in the garden?
Student: *Weeds and grass crowded the little wheat sprouts.*

Instructor: Did anyone help the hen and her chicks pull the weeds?
Student: *No, no one helped them.*

Instructor: Name two other things that needed to be done to the wheat before it could be eaten.
Student: *The wheat needed to be harvested, taken to the thresher to be separated, taken to the miller to be ground into flour, and the bread needed to be made.*

Instructor: Why do you think the hen did not give any bread to the dog, the cat, or the duck?
Student: *They did not help do any of the work.*

Instructor: Who did get to eat the bread?
Student: *The hen and her chicks ate the bread.*

Instructor: Why did the chicks get to share the bread?
Student: *The chicks helped the hen with the work.*

Copywork

Have the student copy some part of the following section of the Little Red Hen's story, depending on his ability. Remind the student how to make quotation marks. Help him place punctuation properly, inside the quotation marks (you need not explain the rule that governs this at this point).

"Who will help pull the grass and weeds out of the garden of wheat?" said the Little Red Hen.

"Not I," said the dog.

"Not I," said the cat.

"Not I," said the duck.

12/9/19

························ **LESSON 41** ······················

Introducing indirect quotations
Copywork: "Not I"
Poem review: "The Little Bird" (Lesson 39)

Notes to Instructor: *Review "The Little Bird" today.*

Reread the story of the Little Red Hen while the student follows along. Ask the student to read each direct quotation. Encourage him to use different voices. Give him all necessary help with unfamiliar words (this is not primarily a reading exercise, so don't frustrate him by having him sound out difficult words). This exercise will reinforce the rule that direct quotations are enclosed in quotation marks.

Instructor: In the story, the Little Red Hen said, "Who will help me take the bag of wheat to the miller, so that he can grind it into flour?" That is a direct quotation. Those are the actual words said by the Little Red Hen. But if I said "The Little Red Hen wanted to know who would help her take the bag of wheat to the miller," I am changing the Little Red Hen's actual words into my own words. That is no longer a direct quotation. A *direct* quotation is the actual words that a person says. An *indirect* quotation tells you what a person says, without using his or her actual words. Read this direct quotation from the Little Red Hen with me:

"Who will help me plant this wheat?"

Note to Instructor: *Show the student this quotation and point out the quotation marks around it. Go back to the story and show the student this quotation in the second paragraph. Point out that these are the Little Red Hen's actual words.*

Instructor: Now I will tell you what the Little Red Hen said by using an indirect quotation:

The Little Red Hen asked someone to help her plant wheat.

Note to Instructor: *Show the student the sentence above. Point out that there are no quotation marks around the words.*

Instructor: This is the same information, but not the actual words of the Little Red Hen, so we do not put quotation marks around these words. Now I want you to read me some direct quotations. I will turn them into indirect quotations. Follow along with me as we read together.

Note to Instructor: *Allow the student to read the following script along with you. Use your finger to help him follow.*

Student reads: "Who will help pull the grass and weeds out of the garden of wheat?"

Instructor: The Little Red Hen wanted to know who would help her weed the garden.

Student reads: "Not I," said the dog.

Instructor: The dog said that he would not help.

Student reads: "Who will help me harvest the wheat?"

Instructor: The Little Red Hen asked for help harvesting the wheat.

Student reads: "Not I," said the cat.

Instructor: The cat said that he would not help either.

Student reads: "Who will help me bake some bread?"

Instructor: The Little Red Hen wondered if anyone would help her bake bread.

Student reads: "Not I," said the duck.

Instructor: The duck also said that he would not help.

Instructor: Remember, a direct quotation has quotation marks around it to show the actual words that a person (or a duck) says. An indirect quotation does not use a person's actual words. Indirect quotations have no quotation marks.

Copywork

Choose one of the sentence pairs below. Point out that the first sentence is a direct quotation, and the second is an indirect quotation.

"Not I."

The dog said that he wouldn't help.

"Who will help me bake some bread?"

The Little Red Hen wanted help baking her bread.

"Who will help pull the grass and weeds out of the garden of wheat?"

The Little Red Hen wanted to know who would help her weed the garden.

12/13/19

•   **LESSON 42**   • • • • • • • • • • • • • • • • • •

Titles of respect
Adjectives
Quotation marks
Dictation exercise: "Who will help me?"

Instructor: Let's review one of the lessons we've already learned. Do you remember what a title of respect is? It is a word, like "Mr.," "Mrs.," "Dr.," or "Miss," that goes in front of a person's name. We usually abbreviate these titles of respect. Let's look together at these titles and their abbreviations.

Note to Instructor: *Show the student the following chart of titles and abbreviations. Read through it as the student follows along.*

Mister	Mr.	This is a title for a man.
Mistress	Mrs.	This is a title for a married woman.
Doctor	Dr.	This is a title for a physician or for someone with a special degree from a university.
Miss	—	This is not an abbreviation, but a title of courtesy for an unmarried girl or woman.
*	Ms.	Ms. is an abbreviation for either Mistress or Miss. You should use it when you do not know whether a woman would prefer to be called Mrs. or Miss.

Instructor: Abbreviated titles of respect begin with capital letters and end with periods. Copy the abbreviations "Mr.," "Mrs.," "Dr.," and "Ms." onto your paper now. Also copy "Miss."

Note to Instructor: *Allow the student to look at the book while he copies. Remind him that "Miss" does not have a period because it is not actually an abbreviation.*

Instructor: Now let's review another lesson. Do you remember the definition of an adjective?

Note to Instructor: *Give the student a chance to remember the definition. Praise him if he can remember it! If he cannot, remind him: An adjective is a word that describes a noun.*

Instructor: Let's repeat the definition of an adjective together twice.

TOGETHER (two times): **An adjective is a word that describes a noun.**

Instructor: Can you think of five adjectives that tell what color something is?

> **Note to Instructor:** *Prompt student, if necessary: yellow, blue, red, green, white, black, brown, orange, maroon, purple, violet, tan, pink.*

Instructor: Now, can you think of five adjectives that tell what size something is?

> **Note to Instructor:** *Prompt student, if necessary: big, small, short, tall, wide, narrow, huge, little, tiny, enormous, fat, thin.*

Instructor: Now, can you think of four adjectives to describe something in this room? I will write the adjectives down while you say them.

> **Note to Instructor:** *Help the student think of descriptive words for an object in the room. Write the adjectives down. Then help him to form them into a sentence: "The [object] is [adjective], [adjective], [adjective], and [adjective]." Write the sentence down and point out the commas that separate the adjectives. These adjectives are items in a series.*

Instructor: For the last part of your lesson today, we will review quotation marks. Remember, a direct quotation has quotation marks around it to show the actual words that a person says. An indirect quotation does not use a person's actual words. Indirect quotations have no quotation marks.

Here is a direct quotation:
"Who will eat this loaf?" asked the Little Red Hen.

Here is an indirect quotation:
The Little Red Hen wanted to know who would eat the loaf.

> **Note to Instructor:** *Show the student the sentences above. Point out the quotation marks around the direct quotation. Point out that the indirect quotation has no quotation marks.*

Instructor: Now you read the direct quotations below, and I will read the indirect quotations. Follow along with me as we read.

Student reads: "I will!" said the dog.

Instructor: The dog said that he would eat some bread.

Student reads: "No, you won't!" said the Little Red Hen.

Instructor: The Little Red Hen said that the dog could not eat the bread.

Student reads: "My chicks and I will eat it together."

Instructor: The Little Red Hen said that she and the chicks would eat the bread.

Dictation Exercise

Tell the student that you will dictate a direct quotation. Remind the student that quotation marks should go on either side of the direct quotation. Choose one of the direct quotations below. If you choose the last sentence, remind the student that you will pause at the comma.

"Who will help me eat this loaf?"

"Who will help me take the bag of wheat to the miller?"

"You would not help us make the bread, so you cannot help us eat the bread."

12/16/19

••••••••••••••••••••• **LESSON 43** •••••••••••••••••••

Four types of sentences
Dictation exercise: "The dump truck"
Poem review: "The Little Bird" (Lesson 39)

Note to Instructor: *Review "The Little Bird" today.*

Instructor: Let's review the definition of a sentence. Listen first, and then repeat with me: **A sentence is a group of words that expresses a complete thought**.

TOGETHER: **A sentence is a group of words that expresses a complete thought**.

Instructor: Repeat with me: **All sentences begin with a capital letter and end with a punctuation mark**.

TOGETHER: **All sentences begin with a capital letter and end with a punctuation mark**.

Instructor: There are four types of sentences. Can you remember what they are?

Note to Instructor: *Give the student time to think and remember before reminding him.*

Instructor: The four types of sentences are statement, command, question, and exclamation. Let's review those definitions. Repeat with me: **Statements give information**.

TOGETHER: **Statements give information**.

Instructor: Statements end with periods. Can you make a statement that gives me information about something in this room?

Note to Instructor: *If necessary, prompt the student with a question: "Can you tell me where the book is? The book is on the table. That is a statement."*

Instructor: Let's say the definition of a command together: **A command gives an order or makes a request**.

TOGETHER: **A command gives an order or makes a request**.

Instructor: Can you give me a command?

Note to Instructor: *If the command is reasonable, act out the command after the student gives it.*

Instructor: When you write statements and commands, statements always end with a period.

Commands usually end with a period. Now let's repeat the definition of the third type of sentence: **A question asks something**. Let's say that together.

TOGETHER: **A question asks something**.

Instructor: A question ends with a question mark. Ask me a question, and I will write it down on my paper.

Note to Instructor: *Write the student's question on your paper. Make a question mark at the end, and point out the question mark.*

Instructor: Now let's repeat the last definition: **An exclamation shows sudden or strong feeling.** Say that with me.

TOGETHER: **An exclamation shows sudden or strong feeling.**

Instructor: Do you remember what punctuation mark comes at the end of an exclamation? An exclamation point. I will ask you a question, and I want you to answer it with an exclamation. Do you love your birthday?

Student: *I love my birthday!*

Note to Instructor: *Remind the student to say this with strong feeling. Write the exclamation down on your paper, and show the student the exclamation point.*

Instructor: Let's pretend that we are on a car trip together—a very long car trip. You are the parent, driving the car, and I am the little child in the back seat. I am very tired of riding! I am going to read you some things I might say on this very long, long trip. You follow along. I want you to tell me for each sentence if it is a statement, a question, a command, or an exclamation.

Note to Instructor: *To help the student keep his place, move your finger along above each sentence (or place a paper marker under each line). Laugh and have fun with this lesson.*

Are we there yet?

Can we stop for a hamburger?

Give me an apple, please.

Are we there yet?

My brother is touching me!

How much farther is it?

Can we get some ice cream?

I see an enormous truck with cars on it!

Give me the water, please.

I have to go to the bathroom.

Are we there yet?

I'm tired of wearing my seat belt.

It's hot back here.

Now it's cold back here.

How much farther is it?

Are we there yet?

Dictation Exercise

Choose one or more of the following sentences to dictate to the student. Remind him of the proper punctuation mark for each.

Stop.

Is a car coming?

It isn't a car. It is a dump truck.

The dump truck is full of rocks, and they are falling out!

Enrichment Activity

- The instructor should pretend to be a four-year-old. Have fun with it; talk in a little child's voice. Have the student talk in a "big grown-up's voice." Answers in brackets are only suggestions. Accept any reasonable answer. If the student answers in a fragment, rephrase the information to form a complete sentence and have the student repeat the correct form back to you. For example, if the student answers the first question with just "No," you give the complete sentence "No, we are not there yet." Then have the student repeat the complete sentence after you.

Instructor (pretending to be the child): Are we there yet?
Student (pretending to be the parent): [No, we are not there yet.]

Instructor (pretending to be the child): May we get some ice cream?
Student (pretending to be the parent): [Yes, we will get some soon.]

Instructor (pretending to be the child): Are we there yet?
Student (pretending to be the parent): [No, it will be a while.]

Instructor (in regular voice): Pretending to be a child, I will give a command or request. Pretending to be the parent, you tell whether or not you will do it.

Instructor (pretending to be the child): Read me a story.
Student (pretending to be the parent): [No, I am driving.]

Instructor (pretending to be the child): Stop at a playground, please.
Student (pretending to be the parent): [Yes, I will as soon as I can.]

Instructor (pretending to be the child): Look at those huge mountains!
Student (pretending to be the parent): [Yes, they are big.]

Instructor (in regular voice): If I make a simple statement, answer any way you wish.

Instructor (pretending to be the child): I'm tired of wearing my seat belt.
Student (pretending to be the parent): [You must wear it for safety.]

Instructor (pretending to be the child): I want a sandwich.
Student (pretending to be the parent): [We'll be eating lunch soon.]

Instructor (pretending to be the child): We are going on a picnic.
Student (pretending to be the parent): [I can hardly wait.]

Instructor (in regular voice): If I make an exclamation, you make an exclamation, too!

Instructor (pretending to be the child): Ouch! My seat belt is pinching me!

Student *(pretending to be the parent):* [*Sorry! I'll loosen it for you!*]

Instructor (pretending to be the child): Stop! There is a place to buy a drink!
Student *(pretending to be the parent):* [*Quick! I'll get in the right lane!*]

Instructor (pretending to be the child): Yippee! We are at the park!
Student *(pretending to be the parent):* [*Whew! I'm glad! That traffic was horrible!*]

LESSON 44

Story narration: "The Three Billy Goats Gruff"

Poem review: "The Year" (Lesson 31)

12/18/19

Notes to Instructor: *Review "The Year" today.*

Read aloud the story below. Use a soft, high voice for Little Billy Goat Gruff, a medium voice for Middle-sized Billy Goat Gruff, and a great, big, loud voice for Great Big Billy Goat Gruff. Use a growling, roaring, bellowing voice for the huge, ugly, mean troll. Then ask the "starter questions" at the end of the story. Remember to encourage the student to answer in complete sentences. Then ask the student, "What is one thing you remember from the story?" Write his answer down and read it back to him.

The Three Billy Goats Gruff

A folk tale

Once upon a time three billy goats lived on a hillside. They were Little Billy Goat Gruff, Middle-sized Billy Goat Gruff, and Great Big Billy Goat Gruff.

The three billy goats grazed on their hillside until all the fresh green grass was gone. They decided to cross the stream at the bottom of the hill and go over into the green meadow on the other side. There was plenty of good fresh grass in the meadow, but to cross the stream, they had to go over a rickety-rackety bridge. Under the rickety-rackety bridge lived a huge, ugly, mean, and selfish troll.

The littlest Billy Goat Gruff was the first to cross the bridge. "Trip-trap! Trip-trap!" went the little goat over the bridge.

"Who's that trip-trapping over my bridge?" growled the huge, ugly, mean, and selfish troll.

"It is I, the Little Billy Goat Gruff," said the little goat in a little voice.

"I'm coming to eat you up!" said the troll.

"I'm so little," said the Little Billy Goat Gruff, "I'd hardly be a mouthful for you. Wait for my big brother. He is much fatter than I."

"Be gone, then," snarled the huge, ugly, mean, and selfish troll.

The next day, Middle-sized Billy Goat Gruff started over to the meadow. "TRIP-TRAP! TRIP-TRAP!" went the middle-sized Billy Goat Gruff across the bridge.

"Who's that trip-trapping over my bridge?" roared the troll.

"It is I, Middle-sized Billy Goat Gruff," said the middle-sized goat in a middle-sized voice.

"I'm coming to eat you up!" shouted the huge, ugly, mean, and selfish troll.

"Don't eat me," pleaded the middle-sized billy goat. "Wait for my brother. He is much fatter than I!"

"Be gone, then," growled the troll.

The next day, Great Big Billy Goat Gruff started across the bridge to join his brothers in the meadow. "**TRIP-TRAP! TRIP-TRAP!**" went the Great Big Billy Goat Gruff across the rickety-rackety bridge.

"Who's that trip-trapping over my bridge?" screeched the huge, ugly, mean, and selfish troll.

"**IT IS I, THE GREAT BIG BILLY GOAT GRUFF,**" said Great Big Billy Goat Gruff in his great, big, billy goat voice.

"I'm coming to eat you up!" bellowed the huge, ugly, mean, and selfish troll, and he climbed onto the rickety-rackety bridge.

"**COME ON, THEN,**" said Great Big Billy Goat Gruff.

The Great Big Billy Goat Gruff ran at the huge, ugly, mean, and selfish troll and tossed him into the air with his great big billy goat horns. He tossed the troll so far up the river that the troll never found his way back down.

Now every morning the three Billy Goats Gruff trip-trap across the rickety-rackety bridge to eat sweet green grass or wallow in the fresh meadow. At night, they trip-trap back across the rickety-rackety bridge to sleep peacefully on their hillside.

Instructor:	How many billy goats were there?
Student:	*There were three billy goats.*
Instructor:	What did each look like?
Student:	*One was little, one was medium-sized, and one was really big.*
Instructor:	Who did Little Billy Goat Gruff meet when he crossed the bridge?
Student:	*He met the troll.*
Instructor:	What did the troll want to do to Little Billy Goat Gruff?
Student:	*He wanted to eat him.*

Instructor: Why didn't the troll eat him?

Student: *Little Billy Goat Gruff said that his brother was bigger and the troll should eat him.*

Instructor: What did the troll want to do to Middle-sized Billy Goat Gruff?

Student: *He wanted to eat him.*

Instructor: Why didn't the troll eat him?

Student: *Middle-sized Billy Goat Gruff said his brother was bigger and the troll should eat him.*

Instructor: What did the troll want to do to Great Big Billy Goat Gruff?

Student: *He wanted to eat him.*

Instructor: What did Great Big Billy Goat Gruff say to the troll?

Student: *He said, "Come on, then!"*

Instructor: What did Great Big Billy Goat Gruff do to the troll?

Student: *He tossed him up the river with his horns.*

LESSON 45

Quotations
Four types of sentences
Parts of speech
Conjunctions
Dictation exercise: "I'm coming to eat you up!"

12/19/19

Notes to Instructor: *In Lesson 49, the student will need five or six first-class postcard stamps and postcards to address to relatives. Plan now to have these on hand.*

Instructor: Look back at the story of the Three Billy Goats Gruff with me. Can you point out some quotations? Look at the quotation marks on either side of these quotations. These are the actual words that the goats and the troll used. Here is an indirect quotation from the story: The troll said that he would eat the billy goats. Can you find the troll's exact words and read them for me?

Student: *"I'm coming to eat you up!"*

Instructor: What is your favorite quotation from the story?

Note to Instructor: *Help the student find the answers to the following questions in the story. Depending on the student's reading ability, either you or the student should read the story aloud as you complete the rest of the lesson.*

Instructor: Now can you find me an exclamation? Remember, it will end with an exclamation point. Can you find a question that ends with a question mark? Can you find a command? The troll gives commands to the billy goats, doesn't he? Can you find a statement? Any sentence which tells you what happens next is a statement. Statements end with periods. Now can you find a sentence that has items in a list, separated by commas?

Note to Instructor: *If the student cannot locate the sentence, point out the phrase "the huge, ugly, mean, and selfish troll."*

Instructor: Is the word "troll" a noun, a verb, an adjective, a conjunction, or an interjection?

Note to Instructor: *If necessary, remind the student that a noun is the name of a person, place, thing, or idea.*

Instructor: "Troll" is a noun. Is the troll a person, place, thing, or idea? I think he is either a person or a thing! The words "huge, ugly, mean, and selfish" describe the troll. What do we call words that describe a noun?

Student: *An adjective describes a noun.*

Instructor: "Huge," "ugly," "mean," and "selfish" are all adjectives. Can you find three action verbs in the story of the Billy Goats Gruff?

Note to Instructor: *Action verbs in the story include: grazed, decided, cross, went, growled, said, snarled, roared, shouted, pleaded, screeched, bellowed, tossed, and ran. "Trip-trap" is also used as a verb.*

Instructor: Can you find a linking verb? Look for "am," "is," "are," "was," and "were."

Note to Instructor: *Linking verbs are found in the first paragraph ("They were Little Billy Goat Gruff..."), the second paragraph ("There was plenty of good fresh grass..."), the third paragraph ("The littlest Billy Goat Gruff was the first..."), the fifth paragraph ("It is I..."), etc.*

Instructor: Now let's look for conjunctions. Remember, a conjunction joins words or groups of words together. Look for the words "and," "but," "or."

Dictation Exercise

Choose one or more of the following sentences. Tell the student that these are direct quotations and should have quotation marks around them.

"I'm coming to eat you up!"

"I'd hardly be a mouthful for you."

"Wait for my big brother. He is much fatter than I."

12/20

• • • • • • • • • • • • • • • • • •   **LESSON 46**   • • • • • • • • • • • • • • • • •

Picture narration: "At this the whole pack rose up into the air..." by Arthur Rackham

Instructor: Look at the picture while I tell you about the artist, Arthur Rackham. He was born about 150 years ago, in England. Like N. C. Wyeth, he was an illustrator of children's books such as *Peter Pan* and *Rip Van Winkle*. This illustration is from *Alice's Adventures in Wonderland*. Alice has been arguing with the King and Queen of Hearts. She gets angry and tells them that they're "nothing but a pack of cards." This picture shows what happened next! What are all of the cards doing?

Student: *The cards are flying all over Alice.*

Instructor: Look at the cards at the top of the page. Then look at the cards in the middle and at the bottom. How are they different?

Student: *The cards in the middle and bottom have faces, hands, and feet. The cards at the top are just cards.*

Instructor: Alice looks very surprised. How can you tell that she is surprised?

Student: *She looks surprised because she is throwing up her hands.*

Instructor: What kind of interjection might Alice have said, to show that she was surprised?

Student: *"Oh, no!" [or another appropriate interjection]*

Instructor: What other characters can you see in the picture?

Student: *There is a mouse, a salamander [or lizard], a frog, and a bird.*

Instructor: Spend a few more minutes looking at the picture while I read the description of the King and Queen of Hearts, from *Alice's Adventures in Wonderland* by Lewis Carroll.

"First came ten soldiers carrying clubs; these were all...oblong and flat, with their hands and feet at the corners: next the ten courtiers; these were ornamented all over with diamonds, and walked two and two, as the soldiers did. After these came the royal children; there were ten of them, and the little dears came jumping merrily along hand in hand, in couples: they were all ornamented with hearts. Next came the guests, mostly Kings and Queens, and among them Alice recognised the White Rabbit: it was talking in a hurried, nervous manner, smiling at everything that was said, and went by without noticing her. Then followed the Knave of Hearts, carrying the King's crown on a crimson velvet cushion; and, last of all this grand procession, came THE KING AND QUEEN OF HEARTS."

Note to Instructor: *You can view this painting and others from Arthur Rackham's illustration of* Alice's Adventures in Wonderland *in a number of internet archives, including http://www.bugtown.com/alice and http://www.guiascostarica.com/alicia/ar_img.htm.*

••••••••••••••••••••• **LESSON 47** •••••••••••••••••••••

Introducing adverbs
Dictation exercise: "I ate my supper"
Poem review: "The Year" (Lesson 31)

1/6/19

Note to Instructor: *Review "The Year" today.*

Instructor: An adjective is a word that describes a noun. When you describe a noun, you tell more about it. The word "baby" is just a noun. But if you describe a baby as hungry, fat, happy, and squirmy, you can picture that baby in your mind! Just as we use descriptive words to tell more about nouns, we also use descriptive words to tell more about verbs. A word that describes a verb is called an adverb. Can you hear the word "verb" in the word "adverb"? That will help you to remember that an adverb is a word that describes a verb. Imagine that the hungry, fat, happy, squirmy baby is crying. How is he crying? Loudly? Softly? Angrily? Frantically? Demandingly? All of those words are adverbs. Each adverb describes the verb "crying." Each adverb tells you more about how the baby is crying. Most adverbs end with the letters "-ly." Here is the definition of an adverb: **An adverb is a word that describes a verb, an adjective, or another adverb.** I will say that again for you, and then we will repeat it together three times. **An adverb is a word that describes a verb, an adjective, or another adverb.**

TOGETHER (three times): **An adverb is a word that describes a verb, an adjective, or another adverb.**

Instructor: Today we will talk about adverbs that describe verbs. I will give you some verbs. Let's try to think of adverbs that describe them. First, we will talk about the verb "work." Think of a word that describes how you can work.

Note to Instructor: *Suggestions for adverbs include: carefully, carelessly, slowly, eagerly, reluctantly, cheerfully, grumpily, thoughtfully, energetically.*

Instructor: Let's think of adverbs to describe the verb "eat."

Note to Instructor: *Suggestions for adverbs include: neatly, sloppily, hungrily, carefully, slowly, eagerly, messily, politely, greedily, daintily, gratefully.*

Instructor: Let's think of adverbs to describe the verb "dance."

Note to Instructor: *Suggestions for adverbs include: rhythmically, gracefully, skillfully, awkwardly, clumsily, slowly, quickly, energetically, nimbly, happily, joyfully, frantically, merrily.*

Instructor: Answer the following questions by using adverbs. Try to answer me in complete sentences! If I say "How did the child cry?" you should answer "The child cried noisily," or "The child cried angrily." How did the dancer dance?

Student: *The dancer danced [gracefully].*

Instructor: How did the careless driver drive?
Student: *The careless driver drove [dangerously].*

Instructor: How did the little girl write her name?
Student: *The little girl wrote her name [neatly].*

Instructor: How did John do his work?
Student: *John did his work [quickly].*

Instructor: How did the boy carry his kitten?
Student: *The boy carried his kitten [carefully].*

Instructor: How did the woman decorate the cake?
Student: *The woman decorated the cake [beautifully].*

Note to Instructor: *Additional adverbs that you may use to prompt the student in any of the above sentences include: cheaply, recklessly, clearly, dearly, diligently, beautifully, happily, strangely, unexpectedly, loudly, swiftly, softly, sweetly, gently, smoothly, bitterly, sadly, angrily, quietly, easily, immediately.*

Instructor: I will say the definition of an adverb again for you, and then we will repeat it together three more times. **An adverb is a word that describes a verb, an adjective, or another adverb.**

TOGETHER (three times): **An adverb is a word that describes a verb, an adjective, or another adverb.**

Dictation Exercise

Choose one or more of the following sentences. If you choose the sentence with commas, remember to pause when you reach each comma.

I ate my supper gratefully.

I drank my milk thirstily and ate my sandwich carefully.

I ate my lunch hungrily, asked for my dessert politely, and waited for it patiently.

• • • • • • • • • • • • • • • • • • •   LESSON 48   • • • • • • • • • • • • • • • •

Adverbs
Dictation exercise: "Whole Duty of Children"
Poem review: "The Little Bird" (Lesson 39)

Notes to Instructor: *In Lesson 49, the student will need five or six first-class postcard stamps and postcards to address to relatives. Plan now to have these on hand. You will also need the addresses of several friends and family members.*

Review "The Little Bird" today.

Instructor: I will say the definition of an adverb again for you, and then we will repeat it together three more times. **An adverb is a word that describes a verb, an adjective, or another adverb.**

TOGETHER (three times): **An adverb is a word that describes a verb, an adjective, or another adverb.**

Instructor: We have practiced finding adverbs that describe verbs. Let's practice that one more time. Can you list adverbs that describe the verb "talk"?

Note to Instructor: *Suggestions for adverbs include: loudly, softly, incessantly, rarely, clearly, happily, swiftly, sweetly, gently, sadly, quietly.*

Instructor: An adverb is a word that describes a verb. Now let's talk about the second part of that definition: An adverb is a word that describes an adjective. Imagine that you see a black horse, galloping across a field. You might say "That is a beautiful horse." But if the horse is the most beautiful horse you have ever seen, you might say "That is a very beautiful horse." "Very" tells you just how beautiful the horse is. "Very" is an adverb because it describes the word "beautiful." It doesn't describe the horse. It is not a "very horse"! It is "very beautiful." I will read some sentences to you. Let's try together to find the adjective in each sentence and the adverb that describes it. "It is an extremely hot day." "Day" is a noun. What kind of day is it?

Student: *It is a hot day.*

Instructor: "Hot" is an adjective that describes the noun "day." "It is an extremely hot day." What word tells you how hot it is?

Student: *Extremely.*

Instructor: "Extremely" is an adverb that describes the adjective "hot." Listen to this sentence. "This is a perfectly beautiful flower!" What word describes the noun "flower"?

Student: *Beautiful.*

Instructor:	"Beautiful" is an adjective that describes "flower." "This is a perfectly beautiful flower." How beautiful is the flower?
Student:	*The flower is perfectly beautiful.*

Instructor:	"Perfectly" is an adverb that describes how beautiful the flower is. It describes the adjective "beautiful." Here is one last sentence: "The baby is unusually noisy today." What is the baby?
Student:	*The baby is noisy.*

Instructor:	"Noisy" is an adjective that describes the baby. How noisy is the baby?
Student:	*The baby is unusually noisy.*

Instructor:	"Unusually" is an adverb that tells you more about the adjective "noisy." It doesn't describe the baby—the baby isn't an "unusually baby"! "Unusually" describes "noisy." Let's repeat the definition of an adverb together again: **An adverb is a word that describes a verb, an adjective, or another adverb.** We have talked about adverbs that describe verbs, and adverbs that describe adjectives. Sometimes, adverbs describe other adverbs! Listen to this last sentence: "The dog howled incredibly loudly." In this sentence, "loudly" is an adverb. It tells you more about the verb "howled." How did the dog howl?
Student:	*The dog howled loudly.*

Instructor:	There is another adverb in this sentence. "Incredibly" describes "loudly." It tells you just how loudly the dog howled! "Incredibly" is an adverb that describes another adverb—"loudly." Let's repeat our definition together one last time: **An adverb is a word that describes a verb, an adjective, or another adverb.**

TOGETHER:	**An adverb is a word that describes a verb, an adjective, or another adverb.**

Dictation Exercise

Dictate as much of the following poem as fits the student's writing ability. A single line is acceptable! Show the poem to the student. Remind him that each line of poetry begins with a capital letter. Point to the end of each line. Explain that punctuation at the end of a line of poetry doesn't follow any particular rule. Show the student that there are commas at the end of each line, and a period at the end. Then dictate the poem, giving the student any necessary help in spelling, and remind him of the proper punctuation for the end of each line.

Whole Duty of Children
By Robert Louis Stevenson

A child should always say what's true,
And speak when he is spoken to,
And behave mannerly at table,
At least as far as he is able.

. . . .   **LESSON 49**   . . . .

Addresses

Copywork: Addressing Postcards

Note to Instructor: *The student will need five or six first-class postcard stamps and postcards for this lesson as well as the addresses for family members and close friends.*

Instructor: **An adverb is a word that describes a verb, an adjective, or another adverb**. Let's say that together three times.

TOGETHER (three times): **An adverb is a word that describes a verb, an adjective, or another adverb.**

Instructor: Adverbs describe verbs, adjectives, and other adverbs; adjectives describe nouns. Do you remember the definition of an adjective? Let's say it together three times: **An adjective is a word that describes a noun.**

TOGETHER (three times): **An adjective is a word that describes a noun.**

Instructor: Today we are going to practice writing names and addresses. Do you remember talking about the first, middle, and last names of people in our family? These special names are proper nouns. Let's write down the first, middle, and last names of three people in our family. We will be sending postcards to them a little later on.

Note to Instructor: *Write down the first, middle, and last names of these family members. You could also include close friends to whom the student might wish to send a postcard. Leave enough space under each name to write an address. If you don't know the middle name, write the person's title of respect (Mr. John Knowles, for example), and remind the student that abbreviated titles of respect begin with a capital letter and end with a period.*

Instructor: We will write the names and addresses of these people on postcards. Postcards are like little letters. There is just enough room to write a sentence or two! Each postcard needs a full address, so that the post office can deliver it to the right house. I will write down our address so that we can review the different parts of an address.

Note to Instructor: *As you write your address for the student, remind him what each part stands for. Review street or house number, street name, city name, and the proper state abbreviation. Remind him that state abbreviations are two capitalized letters with no period after them. Write your ZIP code, and remind him that a ZIP code is a special number that helps the post office find where you live.*

Instructor: Now, I will write for you the addresses of some of the people whose names we've written down.

Note to Instructor: *Write three to five addresses underneath the names you have previously written. As you write, explain each abbreviation and part of the address to the student.*

Copywork

If the postcards for this lesson do not already have address lines on them, draw lines for the student to write on (see Lesson 37). Ask the student to address as many postcards as his writing ability allows. Try to have the student address at least one postcard. He will be adding messages to these postcards in a later lesson. The instructor may write the return address.

· · · · · · · · · · · · · · · ·   **LESSON 50**   · · · · · · · · · · · · · · · · · ·

1/16/20

Writing postcards
Nouns
Adjectives
Copywork: Writing Postcards
Poem review: "The Goops" (Lesson 2)

Notes to Instructor: *The student will need the postcards from the previous lesson.*

Review "The Goops" today.

Instructor: Today we are going to write messages on our postcards. To write these messages, we will need nouns and adjectives. Let's review the definition of a noun. **A noun is the name of a person, place, thing, or idea.** Repeat that definition for me.

Student: *A noun is the name of a person, place, thing, or idea.*

Instructor: **An adjective is a word that describes a noun.** Let's repeat that together three times.

Together (three times): **An adjective is a word that describes a noun.**

Instructor: Your postcard message can be about a person, a place, or a thing. You can also write a message about an animal. Remember, the names of animals are nouns too! I would like you to tell me the name of a friend, brother, or sister; the name of a place where you have been recently; the name of a thing, like a toy or book, that you have enjoyed; and the name of an animal, either a pet or an animal you find interesting.

Note to Instructor: *Help the student come up with these nouns. If he has trouble thinking of a place, suggest the grocery store, a playground, a place of worship, or some other place that you have visited in the past two weeks. Write the nouns that the student suggests on a piece of paper, so that he can look at them.*

Instructor: Now I want you to think of an adjective that best describes each one of these nouns.

Note to Instructor: *Your goal is to help the student think through a sentence that he will write on each postcard. The sentence should contain a noun and a word or phrase that describes the noun. You may use the following questions to help the student think of a descriptive word or phrase: What is the most important thing about this person? What is the most interesting thing about this place? Why do you like to play with this toy or read this book? What will help another person picture the animal in their mind? Focus on the person, place, thing, or animal that he is best able to describe. Help him formulate a sentence that tells another person why he finds this particular noun so interesting. Your goal is for the student to complete at least one sentence that he would like to share with someone else and will enjoy sending through the mail on a postcard. This sentence might be, "My baby sister is cute!" "We went to a fun playground." "I like my new Legos™ because it is fun to build with them." "Our dog has five tiny puppies." "My baby sister has a new tooth!" Any* *of these sentences would be a good piece of news for a postcard. So would "We played at a playground with a great curvy slide," or "I read an exciting book last week. It was called _____." Write the student's final, favorite sentence or sentences on a sheet of paper.*

Copywork

Ask the student to copy his favorite sentence or sentences from your paper onto his postcards. Try to complete at least one postcard. Give him any help necessary to make this legible! You may want to allow him to use a pen, or trace over his pencil writing afterwards yourself; pencil sometimes smears in the mail. Mail the postcards with first-class stamps; they will arrive sooner!

1/22/20

••••••••••••••••••••• **LESSON 51** •••••••••••••••••••••

Dates
Months of the year
Seasons
Days of the week
Copywork: Remembering the days of the week

Note to Instructor: *The student will need construction paper and art supplies for the enrichment activity.*

Instructor: What is today's date? Let's write it now.

Note to Instructor: *Write today's date. Point out the comma between the day of the month and the year.*

Instructor: Each part of this date gives us information. The month tells us the season. Let's review the poem "The Year," which tells us what happens in each month.

Note to Instructor: *Ask the student to recite "The Year." Prompt him, if necessary.*

The Year
Sara Coleridge, adapted by Sara Buffington

January brings the snow,
Helps the skis and sleds to go.

February brings the rain,
Thaws the frozen lake again.

March brings breezes loud and shrill,
Stirs the dancing daffodil.

April brings the primrose sweet,
Scatters daisies at our feet.

May brings sunshine full and bright,
Sends the busy bees to flight.

June brings tulips, lilies, roses,
Fills the children's hands with posies.

Hot July brings stormy showers,
Lemonade, and lazy hours.

August brings the warmest air,
Sandy feet and sea-wet hair.

September brings the fruits so sweet,
Apples ripe from summer heat.

October brings the colored trees,
Scampering squirrels and cooling breeze.

Dull November brings the blast,
Then the leaves are whirling fast.

Chill December brings the sleet,
Blazing fire, and Christmas treat.[1]

1 An alternate last line: "Blazing fire, and winter treat."

Instructor: The year has four seasons: winter, spring, summer, and fall. We capitalize the names of the months, but we do not capitalize the names of the seasons. What are the winter months? Can you tell me in a complete sentence?

Note to Instructor: *Prompt the student for the answers to the following questions, if necessary.*

Student: *The winter months are December, January, and February.*

Instructor: What are the spring months?
Student: *The spring months are March, April, and May.*

Instructor: What are the summer months?
Student: *The summer months are June, July, and August.*

Instructor: What are the fall months?
Student: *The fall months are September, October, and November.*

Instructor: The second part of the date tells you what day of the month it is. I will read you the poem "The Months" that tells us about the number of days in each month.

The Months
Mother Goose rhyme

Thirty days hath September,
April, June, and November;
All the rest have thirty-one,
Except for February alone,

Which has four and twenty-four
Till leap year gives it one day more.

Note to Instructor: *If the student has not memorized this poem previously, take some time to work on memorizing it now.*

Instructor: The last part of the date is the year. What is the year of today's date? In what year were you born? How old are you? Do you know on what day of the week you were born? In old times, people thought that the day on which you were born made you act in a certain way! That's just a fairy tale, but it made a fun poem. I will read you a poem about the days of the week.

Days of the Week
Mother Goose rhyme, adapted by Sara Buffington

Monday's child is fair of face,
Tuesday's child is full of grace;
Wednesday's child is ever so sweet,
Thursday's child is tidy and neat;
Friday's child is prone to a giggle,
Saturday's child is easy to tickle;
But the child that is born on restful Sunday
Is happy and cheerful, and loves to play.

Dictation Exercise

Ask the student to write out the days of the week from memory. You may remind him of the days as he writes. Help him with the spelling of difficult names.

Enrichment Activity

Have the student make a seven-page "My Week" booklet. The book could contain what the student does each day of the week. You or the student will write the name of one day of the week at the top of each sheet of paper. He can draw pictures or write sentences. Start this activity today, and finish it when the student has time. Have the student paste or draw a picture of himself on the cover.

•••••••••••••••••••   **LESSON 52**   •••••••••••••••••••

Four kinds of verbs
Dictation exercise: "Dinosaurs"   1|31|20

Note to Instructor: *You will need three light colors of construction paper, glue or tape, and a marker for the enrichment activity.*

Instructor: Today we are going to review the definition of a verb and talk about the different kinds of verbs. Listen to the definition of a verb. **A verb is a word that does an action, shows a state of being, links two words together, or helps another verb.** Let's say that together three times.

Together (three times): **A verb is a word that does an action, shows a state of being, links two words together, or helps another verb.**

Instructor: The easiest verbs to recognize are action verbs, because they tell about something you can see happening. I will give you some action verbs. Act them out for me! Run, skip, fall, roll, sing, sleep, read, laugh, talk, bark, meow, roar, growl, squeak.

Note to Instructor: *Use as many of these verbs as you choose. Allow the student to act out each verb.*

Instructor: The second part of your definition is "A verb shows a state of being." Remember, we said that state of being verbs are words that don't show any action—they only show that you exist (Lessons 5 and 6)! When you sit perfectly still, you are not jumping, running, crawling, meowing, or giggling. But you are still here! You just are. These are the verbs which tell us that something "just is." The state of being verbs are: am, is, are, was, were, be, being, been. Let's chant those together three times.

Together (three times):
  Am [clap]
  Is [clap]
  Are, was, were [clap]
  Be [clap]
  Being [clap]
  Been [clap] [clap]

Instructor: These are short sentences with state of being verbs: "She is." "You are." "They were." Another kind of verb called a linking verb connects or links a noun or pronoun to another word. I will give you a few sentences with nouns and linking verbs. You add a word after the linking verb that tells me more about the noun. "The worm was…" Can you tell me how the worm felt to your hand when you touched it?

Student: *The worm was slimy [or cold, etc.].*

Instructor: The linking verb "was" connects "worm" with a word that tells us more about the worm. Can you tell me something about a huge eighteen-wheeler truck if I say "The truck is _____"? Tell me how big the truck is, or what color it is.

Student: *The truck is huge [or another appropriate word].*

Instructor: The linking verb "is" connects the truck with the word "_____." Now finish this sentence: "Blowing bubbles in the yard is…"

Student: *Blowing bubbles in the yard is [fun, messy]!*

Instructor: The linking verb "is" connects "blowing bubbles" with the word "_____." What are the bubbles like? Begin your sentence with "The bubbles are…"

Student: *The bubbles are [round, shiny, tiny, enormous, etc.].*

Instructor: The linking verb "are" connects "bubbles" and "_____." Listen again to the definition of a verb: **A verb is a word that does an action, shows a state of being, links two words together, or helps another verb**. We have talked about verbs that do actions, show state of being, and link words together. Let's finish by talking about verbs that help other verbs. We call these helping verbs. Let's say them together three times.

TOGETHER (three times):
Am [clap]
Is [clap]
Are, was, were [clap]
Be [clap]
Being [clap]
Been [clap] [clap]
Have, has, had [clap]
Do, does, did [clap]
Shall, will, should, would, may, might, must [clap] [clap]
Can, could!

Instructor: I will read you some sentences where a helping verb is helping an action verb. Tell me which helping verb you hear.

Note to Instructor: *The helping verbs in the following sentences are italicized. If necessary, emphasize them slightly as you read.*

Instructor: The Tyrannosaurus rex *was* crashing through the underbrush.
Student: *Was.*

Instructor: Tyrannosaurus *had been* sleeping. He woke up hungry!
Student: *Had, been.*

Instructor: Tyrannosaurus thought, "I *am* hoping to find some prey!"
Student: *Am.*

Instructor: He *was* hoping to find a nice Iguanodon or Allosaurus to eat.
Student: *Was.*

Instructor: As he crashed along, he *could* hear something even bigger behind him.
Student: *Could.*

Instructor: He thought, "It *might* be Gigantosaurus!"
Student: *Might.*

Instructor: Tyrannosaurus decided that it *would* be smarter to return to his cave for another nap.
Student: *Would.*

Instructor: Let's repeat the definition of a verb together two more times.

Together (two times): **A verb is a word that does an action, shows a state of being, links two words together, or helps another verb.**

Dictation Exercise

Choose one of the following sentences.

Some dinosaurs were quite large.

Many dinosaurs were plant eaters, but some ate meat.

Tyrannosaurus rex was hoping that he could find a nice dinosaur for a snack.

Enrichment Activity

Repeat activity from Lesson 7: Help the student make a three-link paper chain from three different colors of construction paper that are light enough for the student to clearly see writing on them. The middle link should be yellow or white. While the links are flat, before putting the chain together:
1. Write a linking verb on the yellow or white link.
2. Write a noun or pronoun on another color link.
3. Write an adjective on the third strip of paper. Glue or tape the chain together, showing that the yellow (or white) linking verb "links" a noun or pronoun with an adjective to make a sentence. You could repeat this project writing a noun instead of an adjective for the third link in the chain.

• **LESSON 53** • • • • • • • • • • • • • • • • • • •

Adverbs

Adjectives

Poem review: "The Year" (Lesson 31)

Notes to Instructor: *The student will need art supplies for the enrichment activity. You will need a volume "C" encyclopedia.*

Review "The Year" today.

Instructor: When we talked about nouns, we learned that **a noun is the name of a person, place, thing, or idea.** When we talked about adjectives, we learned that **an adjective is a word that describes a noun.** I am going to give you a noun that names an animal: "kitten." The noun that names "kitten" doesn't tell me anything about the kitten. I don't know what color it is. I don't know how big it is. I don't know what it feels like to touch. I don't know if it is friendly or wild. I need other words to tell me these things. I am going to ask you to pretend you have a kitten. It can look like a real kitten, or like an imaginary kitten that you would never see in real life. I am going to let you describe this kitten using adjectives. **An adjective is a word that describes a noun.** Let's begin with color words. Color words are adjectives, because they help describe nouns. What color is your pretend kitten?

Student: *My kitten is [color].*

Instructor: I am going to write a sentence that will have all of your adjectives in it. I will begin it "My [color]…"

Note to Instructor: *Begin writing a sentence when the student gives you words. You will make a complete sentence about this kitten, writing each part of the sentence as the student decides on it. Do not write the word "kitten" yet, since we will be adding other adjectives. You may use more than one adjective, verb, or adverb if the student wishes. Encourage the student to picture in his mind this extraordinary kitten.*

Instructor: What size is the kitten? Is it big, enormous, gigantic, large, or tiny? These size words are adjectives that describe the size of the kitten. Choose an adjective to describe this kitten and tell me what it is.

Student: *My kitten is [adjective of size].*

Instructor: Now we know the kitten's size and its color. I will add your new adjective to the sentence I am writing. "My [color], [size]…"

Note to Instructor: *Remember to add commas after these adjectives, since there will be more than two.*

Instructor: Now I know the color and size of the kitten, but I need you to think of an another adjective. This time think of an adjective of touch that would describe your kitten—what does this kitten feel like when you hold it? Is it soft, furry, wet, sticky, curly, or fuzzy?

Student: *My kitten is [adjective of touch].*

Instructor: I will add that to your sentence. Now it reads: "My [color], [size], [adjective of touch] kitten…" Repeat that part of the sentence for me.

Student: *"My [color], [size], [adjective of touch] kitten…"*

Instructor: Now I know the color and size of the kitten and I know how it feels, but I don't know what it does. Now I need an action verb to tell me what this kitten does. Is it a kitten that runs, rolls, falls, jumps, eats, sleeps, skates, floats, plays, barks, mews, or roars?

Student: *[action verb]*

Instructor: Here is what I have written: "My [color], [size], [adjective of touch] kitten [action verb]…" Read that much of the sentence back to me.

Student: *"My [color], [size], [adjective of touch] kitten [action verb]…"*

Instructor: Now I know the color and size of the kitten and I know how it feels, and I do know what it does. But I don't know how it does the action. I need an adverb to tell me how the kitten does his action. Remember: **An adverb is a word that describes a verb, an adjective, or another adverb.** How does the kitten [action verb]?

Note to Instructor: *You may offer the student any of these options: loudly, softly, angrily, frantically, carefully, quickly, slowly, eagerly, hungrily, messily, greedily, daintily, gratefully, skillfully, awkwardly, clumsily, energetically, happily, joyfully, merrily, dangerously, recklessly, clearly, beautifully, unexpectedly, swiftly, sweetly, gently, smoothly, quietly, easily, immediately.*

Student: *[adverb]*

Instructor: Here is the sentence I have written: "My [color], [size], [adjective of touch] kitten [action verb] [adverb]." Read that sentence back to me. Now I know what your kitten is like!

Enrichment Activity

Draw, in color, a picture of this imaginary kitten. Look up "cat" in an encyclopedia and talk about adjectives and adverbs that describe the many varieties of cats.

• **LESSON 54** •

Story narration: "The Storm"

Note to Instructor: *Read aloud the story below. Then ask the "starter questions" at the end of the story. Remember to encourage the student to answer in complete sentences. Then ask the student, "What is one thing you remember from the story?" Write his answer down and read it back to him.*

The Storm
By Sara Buffington

The two little boys eagerly pressed their round faces against the large window. They longed to go outside and play. The older boy sweetly asked their mother, "Mommy, may we go outside and play? We would love to ride our bikes today."

The mother joined her sons at the window and gazed at the sky. "Look at the sky," she said softly. "Do you see the low, dark, gray clouds? That means a storm is coming. Let's stay inside this afternoon."

Just then they heard a long, rumbling sound. "I know that sound," the younger boy said quietly. "That's thunder."

They looked cautiously at the dark sky. More loud rumbles of thunder boomed overhead. The two boys looked at their mother anxiously. So she turned on a bright lamp and said cheerfully, "Let's play a game of Chutes and Ladders. We can sit here near the window so we can play and watch the storm."

They were having great fun playing the board game, and barely heard the pitter-patter of little drops of rain on the roof. But soon the pitter-patter sound changed into a loud, continuous thumping. The rain was pouring! They looked out the window and saw sheets of rain battering their car, yard, and street. "Mommy, do you see the little waterfalls running from the roof?" said the older boy. "They are forming big puddles on the ground!"

A flash of bright light pierced the sky. It was lightning! After a few seconds, they heard a crackling sound, quickly followed by a huge boom. The dazzling lightning and rumbling thunder startled the boys. But they were not scared. They were inside a dry, safe room.

The lightning flashed and the thunder rolled. The little boys gazed out of the window. It was exciting to watch the storm, but they were glad to be inside!

"Plink! Plunk! Plink!" They heard a sound like tiny pebbles hitting the roof. The boys peered out through the window and saw little white balls of ice steadily falling from the sky. "That's hail," their mother explained. "The rain freezes in the sky and then it falls to the ground." The boys thought that hail was strange, but fun. Imagine, ice falling from the sky in the middle of summer!

After a while, the noisy hail stopped. The thunder gradually moved away. The lightning flashed, but it was pale and distant. The rain faded into a light drizzle. The sky grew lighter and lighter. Soon, the sun came out and shone down on the wet grass and enormous puddles.

"Boys," their mother said, "you may go outside and play now."

"Hurrah!" the boys cheered. "But let's watch another summer storm tomorrow!"

Instructor: Why did the boys want to go outside?
Student: *They wanted to ride their bikes.*

Instructor: Why didn't their mother let them go outside?
Student: *She saw a storm coming.*

Instructor: What sound did they hear that first warned them of the storm?
Student: *They heard the thunder.*

Instructor: What was the next thing they heard after the thunder?
Student: *They heard the rain fall.*

Instructor: What did they see when they looked outside?
Student: *They saw lightning and rain.*

Instructor: What fell from the sky that made a "plink" sound on the roof?
Student: *Hail fell from the sky.*

Instructor: How did they know when the storm was over?
Student: *The thunder and lightning stopped, the rain and hail stopped, the sky got lighter, and the sun came out.*

Instructor: Do you think the boys liked watching the storm?
Student: *Yes, they liked watching the storm, but they were glad they watched it from inside the house.*

•   **LESSON 55**   • • • • • • • • • • • • • • • • • • •

Adjectives
Adverbs

Instructor: Can you repeat the definition of an adverb for me?

Student: *An adverb is a word that describes a verb, an adjective, or another adverb.*

Note to Instructor: *If the student cannot remember the definition, repeat it with him three times.*

Instructor: Can you repeat the definition of an adjective for me?

Student: *An adjective is a word that describes a noun or pronoun.*

Note to Instructor: *If the student cannot remember the definition, repeat it with him three times.*

Instructor: Let's look back at the story "The Storm" together (Lesson 54). We will see whether we can find the adjectives and adverbs in this story.

Note to Instructor: *Expect this activity to take the remainder of your lesson time. See the key for the instructor that follows. Ask the student to identify only those adverbs ending in "-ly." When appropriate, point out the noun or pronoun which each adjective describes, and the verb or adjective described by each adverb (you do not need to point this out for every adjective and adverb!). Some adjectives and adverbs (such as "their" and "outside") are not labelled because they have not yet been taught. The purpose of the exercise is to begin to make the student aware of these descriptive words in stories. You need not cover the whole story; spend an appropriate amount of time for your student's attention span.*

Key for the Instructor

   adj. adj.   adv.   adj.   adj.
The two little boys eagerly pressed their round faces against the large window. They longed

          adj.   adv.
to go outside and play. The older boy sweetly asked their mother, "Mommy, may we go outside

and play? We would love to ride our bikes today."

                                                                 adv.
The mother joined her sons at the window and gazed at the sky. "Look at the sky," she said softly.

          adj.   adj.   adj.
"Do you see the low, dark, gray clouds? That means a storm is coming. Let's stay inside this

afternoon."

                          adj.   adj.   adj.

Just then they heard a long, rumbling sound. "I know that sound," the younger boy

    adv.

said quietly. "That's thunder."

                adv.   adj.   adj.   adj.

They looked cautiously at the dark sky. More loud rumbles of thunder boomed overhead.

  adj.   adv.   adj.

The two boys looked at their mother anxiously. So she turned on a bright lamp and said

  adv.

cheerfully, "Let's play a game of Chutes and Ladders. We can sit here near the window so we

can play and watch the storm."

              adj.   adj.   adv.   adj.

They were having great fun playing the board game, and barely heard the pitter-patter of little

                        adj.   adj.   adj.

drops of rain on the roof. But soon the pitter-patter sound changed into a loud, continuous

thumping. The rain was pouring! They looked out the window and saw sheets of rain battering

                                            adj.

their car, yard, and street. "Mommy, do you see the little waterfalls running from the roof ?" said

  adj.   adj.

the older boy. "They are forming big puddles on the ground!"

          adj.   adj.

A flash of bright light pierced the sky. It was lightning! After a few seconds, they heard a

adj.   adv.   adj.   adj.   adj.

crackling sound, quickly followed by a huge boom. The dazzling lightning and rumbling

                                          adj. adj.

thunder startled the boys. But they were not scared. They were inside a dry, safe room.

                                      adj.

The lightning flashed and the thunder rolled. The little boys gazed out of the window. It was

exciting to watch the storm, but they were glad to be inside!

                               adj.

"Plink! Plunk! Plink!" They heard a sound like tiny pebbles hitting the roof. The boys peered

                     adj.   adj.   adv.

out through the window and saw little white balls of ice steadily falling from the sky. "That's hail," their mother explained. "The rain freezes in the sky and then it falls to the ground." The boys

                adj.   adj.

thought that hail was strange, but fun. Imagine, ice falling from the sky in the middle of summer!

           adj.   adv.

After a while, the noisy hail stopped. The thunder gradually moved away. The lightning flashed,

adj.   adj.   adj.   adj.   adj.

but it was pale and distant. The rain faded into a light drizzle. The sky grew lighter and lighter.

                            adj.   adj.

Soon, the sun came out and shone down on the wet grass and enormous puddles.

"Boys," their mother said, "you may go outside and play now."

                        adj.   adj.

"Hurrah!" the boys cheered. "But let's watch another summer storm tomorrow!"

••••••••••••••••••••••• **LESSON 56** •••••••••••••••••••••

Introducing articles
Dictation exercise: "What we did"

2/6

Note to Instructor: *You will need a story book, magazine article, or newspaper column for the enrichment activity.*

Instructor: We have learned about many different kinds of words. We have learned about nouns, verbs, adjectives, adverbs, interjections, and conjunctions. Conjunctions are the shortest of all of those words! Do you remember what a conjunction does? It joins words or groups of words together. The conjunctions are "and," "but," "or." How many letters are in the conjunction "and"? How about "but"? How about "or"?

Note to Instructor: *If necessary, write "and, but, or" and let the student count the letters.*

Instructor: Now we are going to learn about words that are even shorter than conjunctions! These words are called **articles. The articles are "a," "an," and "the."** Let's say that together three times: **The articles are "a," "an," and "the."**

Together (three times): **The articles are "a," "an," and "the."**

Instructor: You use articles whenever you talk about nouns. You use them automatically—you don't even realize that you're using them.

Note to Instructor: *Point to a chair.*

Instructor: What is this?
Student: *A chair [or the chair].*

Note to Instructor: *Most children will automatically use an article. If your student simply says "chair," say, "a chair" and have him repeat it after you.*

Instructor: "A" [or "the"] is an article. We usually use "a" or "an" when we are talking about any old noun, and "the" when we are talking about specific nouns. Repeat this sentence after me: "There is a window."
Student: *There is a window.*

Instructor: That could be any window in this house—or in someone else's house. It is not a specific window. It is "a window."

Note to Instructor: *Point to a window as you say the next sentence.*

Instructor: Repeat this sentence after me: "There is the window."

Student: *There is the window.*

Instructor: "The window" is a specific window—that window right there! We use "the" whenever we are talking about a specific noun. When we are talking about any old noun, we use "a" or "an." "A" and "an" mean the same thing, but we use "an" before words that begin with vowels. When you were learning to read, do you remember learning the names of the vowels? The vowels are a, e, i, o, u. Let's say the vowels together:

TOGETHER: A, e, i, o, u.

Instructor: A, e, i, o, u are vowels. Say that with me.

TOGETHER: A, e, i, o, u are vowels.

Instructor: All the other letters of the alphabet are called consonants. Say that with me.

TOGETHER: All the other letters of the alphabet are called consonants.

Instructor: We use "a" before a word that begins with a consonant. If I say "I will give you a banana," I use "a" before "banana" because "banana" begins with "b." "B" is a consonant. We use "an" before a word that begins with a vowel. If I say "I will give you an apple," I use "an" before "apple" because "apple" begins with "a." "A" is a vowel. Now I am going to play the "A-An" riddle game with you. I will ask you a question. When you give me the answer, you will use "an" before words that begin with a, e, i, o, u. You will use "a" before all the words that begin with consonants—all the other letters of the alphabet. What is a huge, gray animal with a long trunk?

Student: *An elephant.*

Instructor: What has a shell on the outside and a yellow yolk on the inside?

Student: *An egg.*

Instructor: What is something that holds ice cream? We carry it around in our hand while we're eating the ice cream, and then eat it along with the last bit of ice cream.

Student: *An ice-cream cone [or a cone].*

Instructor: What is a cat's baby called?

Student: *A kitten.*

Instructor: What fruit has the same name as its color?

Student: *An orange.*

Instructor: What has scales and swims in lakes, rivers, or the ocean?

Student: *A fish.*

Instructor: What do you hold up over your head when it rains?
Student: *An umbrella.*

Instructor: You use "an" before words that begin with vowels, and "a" before words that begin with consonants. Let's repeat the definition of an article three more times: **The articles are "a," "an," and "the."**

Together (three times): **The articles are "a, an," and "the."**

Dictation Exercise

Choose one or more of the sentences below. Ask the student to choose whether "a" or "an" goes before the nouns. If you dictate the sentences with commas, remember to pause at each comma.

We visited (a or an) zoo and saw (a or an) animal.

My sister and I saw (a or an) airplane, (a or an) helicopter, and (a or an) jet.

At the market we bought (a or an) apple, (a or an) orange, (a or an) banana, and (a or an) bunch of grapes.

Enrichment Activity

Find the articles "a" and "an" in a story, magazine, or news column.
Make a list of several articles along with the word that follows them.

210

•••••••••••••••••••••• **LESSON 57** •••••••••••••••••

Articles
Capitalization review

Note to Instructor: *Introduce the idea that you capitalize titles of poems, stories, and books.*

Instructor: Let's name the articles. **The articles are "a," "an," and "the."** Say that with me three times.

TOGETHER (three times): **The articles are "a," "an," and "the."**

Instructor: We use "the" when we talk about specific nouns. We use "a" or "an" to talk about just any nouns. "A" comes before words that begin with a consonant, and "an" comes before words that begin with a vowel. What sits in a tree and says "Who, who, who"?

Student: *An owl.*

Note to Instructor: *Write down "an owl" and show it to the student.*

Instructor: "Owl" starts with "o," and "o" is a vowel; so we use the article "an." What has four legs and barks?

Student: *A dog.*

Note to Instructor: *Write down "a dog" and show it to the student.*

Instructor: "Dog" starts with "d," and "d" is a consonant; so we use the article "a." I will write out another phrase that has "dog" in it. Do you recognize it?

Note to Instructor: *Write "Go, Dog, Go" on the paper.*

Instructor: This is the title of a book. Have you ever read this book? In this title, the word "dog" starts with a special kind of letter. What is it?

Student: *A capital letter.*

Instructor: The words "Go" and "Dog" are both capitalized because they are part of a title. The first word and every important word in a book title are capitalized. What is your favorite book?

Note to Instructor: *Write down the title of the student's favorite book. Capitalize the first word and every other important word (generally, all words except for the articles "a," "an," and "the" and the conjunctions and prepositions of fewer than five letters). Point out the capital letters.*

Instructor: Let's go back and look at the title of the last story we read. What is it called?

Note to Instructor: *Look together at "The Storm" (Lesson 54). Point out the capital letters in the title.*

Instructor: "The" is the first word of the title, so it is capitalized. "Storm" is an important word, so we capitalize it as well. Titles of stories are capitalized, just like titles of books. Titles of poems are capitalized, too. Let's look back at the last poem we memorized.

Note to Instructor: *Look together at "The Little Bird" (Lesson 39). Point out the capital letters.*

Instructor: The titles of poems, stories, and books are capitalized. Let's review some of the other places we use capital letters. Repeat after me: Capitalize proper names of people and places.

Student: *Capitalize proper names of people and places.*

Instructor: Names like "George Washington" and "Minnesota" are proper names, so they are capitalized. Repeat after me: Capitalize the names of days of the week.

Student: *Capitalize the names of days of the week.*

Instructor: What day of the week is it? Write it down and capitalize it.

Note to Instructor: *Help the student spell the day of the week correctly.*

Instructor: What month is it? Write it down and capitalize it. You should capitalize the months of the year.

Note to Instructor: *Help the student spell the month correctly.*

Instructor: What season is it? Is this winter, spring, summer, or fall? Remember: you should not capitalize the name of a season! Write down the name of the season that we are now in, but don't capitalize it.

Note to Instructor: *Help the student identify the season and write it down.*

Instructor: You should capitalize the name of a holiday. "Thanksgiving" and "Independence Day" are both holidays. They should begin with capital letters. Which one would you like to write down?

Note to Instructor: *Help the student spell whichever holiday he chooses. If necessary, remind him that both words in "Independence Day" are capitalized.*

Instructor: Always capitalize the word "I." Write the sentence "Mom and I made cookies."

Remember to capitalize the word "I."

Note to Instructor: *Give all necessary help.*

Instructor: You should always capitalize initials and put periods after them. Write down your own initials.

Note to Instructor: *Give all necessary help.*

Instructor: And remember—always capitalize the first word in a sentence!

Enrichment Activity

Dictate the following book titles to the student, and help him capitalize and spell them correctly.

The Hungry Caterpillar

Cars and Trucks and Things That Go

LESSON 58

Introducing prepositions
Dictation exercise: "Over my head"
Poem review: "The Little Bird" (Lesson 39)

Notes to Instructor: *Review "The Little Bird" today.*

IMPORTANT! Over the next fifteen lessons, the student will be memorizing a very long list of prepositions. As he continues into later grades, he will find a memorized list of prepositions invaluable. As he learns about subjects, objects, and other ways that words function within sentences, he will need to be able to eliminate prepositional phrases before he can identify the central elements in sentences (since the object of a preposition is never the subject, direct object, or indirect object). The inability to recognize prepositions and their objects is one of the greatest stumbling blocks for students in middle-grade grammar. If he takes the time now to learn the prepositions by heart, his later grammar learning will become much simpler. (The student will learn the definition of a preposition as well, but learning the definition is not enough. He should also memorize the list, since not all prepositions follow the definition exactly.)

Instructor: Let's review articles one more time. **The articles are "a," "an," and "the."** Say that with me three times.

TOGETHER (three times): **The articles are "a," "an," and "the."**

Instructor: Articles are short words. Conjunctions—"and," "but," "or"—are short words. Interjections are short words too. Do you remember interjections? **An interjection is a word that expresses sudden or strong feeling**, like "Wow!" or "Great!" Can you say those two interjections for me?

Student: *Wow! Great!*

Instructor: I'm glad you're enjoying your grammar so much, because we are going to learn a new part of speech! **A preposition is a word that shows the relationship of a noun or pronoun to another word in the sentence.** Let's work on that definition together. Repeat the first part with me three times: **A preposition is a word...**

TOGETHER (three times): **A preposition is a word...**

Instructor: Now let's say the second part three times: **...that shows the relationship...**

TOGETHER (three times): **...that shows the relationship...**

Instructor: Now I will say those two parts of the definition together. **A preposition is a word that shows the relationship...** Let's try to repeat that together three times.

TOGETHER (three times): **A preposition is a word that shows the relationship...**

Instructor: Now let's repeat the next part three times. **...of a noun or pronoun...**

TOGETHER (three times): **...of a noun or pronoun...**

Instructor: I will say the whole definition so far. **A preposition is a word that shows the relationship of a noun or pronoun...** Can we say that together three times?

TOGETHER (three times): **A preposition is a word that shows the relationship of a noun or pronoun...**

Instructor: Now for the last part! **...to another word in the sentence.** Let's say that three times.

TOGETHER (three times): **...to another word in the sentence.**

Instructor: Whew! That was a very long definition. Here is the whole thing: **A preposition is a word that shows the relationship of a noun or pronoun to another word in the sentence.** Let's say that whole thing together three times.

TOGETHER (three times): **A preposition is a word that shows the relationship of a noun or pronoun to another word in the sentence.**

Instructor: You have worked so hard on the definition that you need a break! Lie down on the floor and stretch. Now you are on the floor. What is the relationship between you and the floor? You are on the floor. "On" is a preposition. It is showing the relationship between a pronoun—"you"—and another word in the sentence—"the floor." Now I think that you should shake out your arms. Sit up and hold your arms up, up, up. Look up at your hands. Where are your hands?

Student: *My hands are above my head [or over my head or up in the air or in the air].*

Note to Instructor: *You can prompt the student with one of the above, if necessary.*

Instructor: "Above" [or whatever preposition the student uses] is a preposition. It tells about the relationship between your hands and your head [or your hands and the air]. Now you can put your hands down. I think you should take a real break. I think you should crawl beneath the table and hide. Where are you?

Student: *I am under the table.*

Instructor: You are under the table! "Under" is a preposition. It tells about the relationship between you and the table. Remember: **A preposition is a word that shows the relationship of a noun or pronoun to another word in the sentence.**

Dictation Exercise

Choose one of the following sentences. Remember to pause at each comma.

My hands are over my head.

I am hiding under the table, and no one can see me.

I am stretching out on the floor for a rest because I have worked so hard.

2\3

· · · · · · · · · · · · · · · · · ·   **LESSON 59**   · · · · · · · · · · · · · · · · · ·

Prepositions
Poem review: "The Year" (Lesson 31)

Notes to Instructor: *Review "The Year" today.*

You will need a plate, fork, knife, spoon, napkin, and glass for today's lesson.

Instructor: In the last lesson, we learned a very long definition. **A preposition is a word that shows the relationship of a noun or pronoun to another word in the sentence.** I will say the first part of that definition: **A preposition is a word that shows the relationship**... Repeat that with me three times.

TOGETHER (three times): **A preposition is a word that shows the relationship**...

Instructor: Now listen to the last part of the definition: ...**of a noun or pronoun to another word in the sentence.** Let's say that three times.

TOGETHER (three times): ...**of a noun or pronoun to another word in the sentence.**

Instructor: Here is the whole thing: **A preposition is a word that shows the relationship of a noun or pronoun to another word in the sentence.** Let's say that whole thing together three times.

TOGETHER (three times): **A preposition is a word that shows the relationship of a noun or pronoun to another word in the sentence.**

Instructor: Let's practice some more prepositions while we also practice setting the table. You have a plate, silverware, a glass, and a napkin. Answer this question in a complete sentence. Where will you put the plate?

Note to Instructor: *For each of the following questions, have the student carry out the action he describes in his complete sentence.*

Student: *I will put the plate on the table.*

Instructor: The word "on" tells you about the relationship between the plate and the table. "On" is a preposition. The fork goes beside the plate, on the left. Put the fork beside the plate, on the left. "Beside" is a preposition. It tells you about the relationship between the fork and the plate. The knife also goes beside the plate, on the other side. The knife and the fork have the same relationship to the plate. Both are beside it. Neither one is on the plate! The blade of the knife should be turned toward the plate. The blade of the knife has a very particular relationship to the plate! It is toward it—not away from it. Place the spoon beside the knife. What relationship does the spoon have with the knife?

Student: *The spoon is beside the knife.*

Instructor: Now, place the glass on the table, above the knife. The glass has a relationship to the table and a relationship to the knife. The preposition "on" tells about its relationship to the table. The preposition "above" tells about its relationship to the knife. Now we should place the napkin beside the fork, to the left. If you think that a paper napkin might blow away, you can also place it under the fork. Go ahead and do that now. "Under" is a preposition. It tells about the relationship between the fork and the napkin. There are many different prepositions to learn, so we are going to end today's lesson by chanting a few of them: "Aboard, about, above, across." I will repeat that three times, and then we will say it together three times.

Instructor (three times): Aboard, about, above, across.

Together (three times): Aboard, about, above, across.

Enrichment Activity

Using his body, furniture, toys, and/or a cardboard box, the student may act out a few of the following prepositions:

Above, among, behind, below, beneath, beside, between, in, inside, near, on, off, over, under,

underneath, up, upon, with, within

•   **LESSON 60**   •

Picture narration: "The Great Wave off Kanagawa" by Katsushika Hokusai

Instructor: Look at the picture while I tell you about the artist, Katsushika Hokusai (cat-soo-SHE-kah HA-koo-sigh). He lived two hundred years ago in Japan, and his pictures are woodblock prints—he carved the illustration into a block of wood, pressed it down into ink, and then pressed it on the paper. All of the dark places in the picture are made by the raised parts of the block. The white places show where the wood was carved away.

Note to Instructor: *When you read the instructor script, emphasize the prepositions in bold print.*

Instructor: What is in the background of the picture, a long ways away, **behind** the water?
Student: *A mountain is in the background.*

Instructor: That is Mount Fuji, the highest mountain in Japan (and an active volcano!). Hokusai loved Mount Fuji and created over thirty pictures of it. In this picture, Mount Fuji is **beyond** the water. What is **on** Mount Fuji?
Student: *Snow is on Mount Fuji.*

Instructor: What is going **through** the ocean, **on** the surface of the water?
Student: *Boats are on the surface of the water.*

Instructor: Those are traditional fishing boats. What is looming **over** and **above** the boats?
Student: *A huge wave is above the boats.*

Instructor: The fishermen on the boats are steering them **through** the waves. How many boats do you think there are in the picture?
Student: *There are three boats.*

Note to Instructor: *It is a little difficult to see the third boat. The midsection of the boat at the bottom of the picture and the prow on the left-hand side of the picture belong to two different boats.*

Instructor: What do you think the white dots represent?
Student: *The white dots are foam [or bubbles].*

Instructor: How many fishermen are on each boat?
Student: *[Accept any reasonable answer.]*

Note to Instructor: *You can view this painting at the Metropolitan Museum of Art website, http://www.metmuseum.org/toah/ho/10/eaj/ho_JP1847.htm (or search http://www.metmuseum.org for "Hokusai").*

•••••••••••••••••••••   **LESSON 61**   •••••••••••••••••••

Prepositions
Dictation exercise: "Bed in Summer"

Note to Instructor: *The student may want drawing supplies for the enrichment activity.*

Instructor: Let's keep working on our long preposition definition. **A preposition is a word that shows the relationship of a noun or pronoun to another word in the sentence.** I will say the first part of that definition: **A preposition is a word that shows the relationship...** Repeat that with me three times.

TOGETHER (three times): **A preposition is a word that shows the relationship...**

Instructor: Now listen to the last part of the definition: **...of a noun or pronoun to another word in the sentence.** Let's say that three times.

TOGETHER (three times): **...of a noun or pronoun to another word in the sentence.**

Instructor: Here is the whole thing: **A preposition is a word that shows the relationship of a noun or pronoun to another word in the sentence.** Let's say that whole thing together three times.

TOGETHER (three times): **A preposition is a word that shows the relationship of a noun or pronoun to another word in the sentence.**

Instructor: Let's work on our first list of prepositions. I will repeat it three times, and then we will say it together five times.

Instructor (three times): Aboard, about, above, across.

TOGETHER (five times): Aboard, about, above, across.

Instructor: Now I want you to make up some sentences that use these prepositions. I am going to give you two nouns and a preposition. Make up a sentence that uses the preposition to show the relationship between the two nouns. Here is an example. I might give you the nouns "worm" and "hole," and the preposition "in." You might answer, "The worm is in the hole." Or I might give you the nouns "bird" and "trees," and the preposition "above." You would say, "The bird is above the trees." Here are your first nouns and your first preposition: captain, ship, aboard.

Student: *The captain is aboard the ship.*

Instructor: Book, bears, about.
Student: *The book is about the bears.*

Instructor: Sun, ground, above.
Student: *The sun is above the ground.*

Instructor: Goat, bridge, across.
Student: *The goat ran across the bridge.*

Instructor: Now we will work on the second part of the preposition list. Listen to me say it three times, and then we will try to say it together three times.

Instructor (three times): After, against, along, among, around, at.

Together (three times): After, against, along, among, around, at.

Instructor: Now I will say the whole list that we have learned so far: "aboard, about, above, across, after, against, along, among, around, at." I am going to say that list for you three times. I want you to say as much of it as you can along with me.

Instructor (slowly, three times, with student joining in): Aboard, about, above, across. After, against, along, among, around, at.

Instructor: Let's go on making up sentences together. I am going to give you two words or phrases that you can link together with your preposition: puppy, ball, after.

Note to Instructor: *Give the student any necessary help to formulate sentences like these.*

Student: *The puppy ran after the ball.*

Instructor: Ladder, wall, against.
Student: *The ladder leans against the wall.*

Instructor: Train, tracks, along.
Student: *The train runs along the tracks.*

Instructor: Child, pillows, among.
Student: *The child wallowed among the pillows.*

Instructor: Monkey, mulberry bush, around.
Student: *All around the mulberry bush, the monkey chased the weasel!*

Instructor: Hungry man, table, at.
Student: *The hungry man sat at the table.*

Instructor: Good! Now let's say the whole list together, three more times.

TOGETHER (slowly, three times): Aboard, about, above, across. After, against, along, among, around, at.

Dictation Exercise

Choose the title and one of the following sentences from the first stanza of "Bed in Summer" by Robert Louis Stevenson. Before dictating the stanza, show it to the student. Point out that the important words in the title are capitalized. Show the student that the first word of every line is capitalized. Point out that there is no punctuation mark after the first line, a period after the second line, a comma after the third line, and a period after the last line. Remind the student of this punctuation while dictating.

Bed in Summer
By Robert Louis Stevenson

In winter I get up at night

And dress by yellow candle light.

In summer, quite the other way,

I have to go to bed by day.

Enrichment Activity

Ask the student to make up additional sentences with several of the prepositions from this lesson, following the same pattern. You write each sentence on the top of an unlined piece of paper. Have the student draw the relationship between the nouns and prepositions in the sentence. Stick figures are fine! Then ask the student to write the preposition on the picture at the appropriate place. (For example, you might write "The train runs along the tracks" at the top of the paper. After drawing the train and the tracks, the student could write "along" next to the tracks, or draw an arrow pointing to the train's wheels and write "along" beside the arrow.) As a variation, the student may simply choose to illustrate the sentences given in the lesson.

•   **LESSON 62**   • • • • • • • • • • • • • • • • • •

Prepositions
Dictation exercise: "Beneath the pyramids"

Instructor: Let's review our preposition definition. **A preposition is a word that shows the relationship of a noun or pronoun to another word in the sentence.** I will say the first part of that definition: **A preposition is a word that shows the relationship...** Repeat that with me three times.

TOGETHER (three times): **A preposition is a word that shows the relationship...**

Instructor: Now listen to the last part of the definition: **...of a noun or pronoun to another word in the sentence.** Let's say that three times.

TOGETHER (three times): **...of a noun or pronoun to another word in the sentence.**

Instructor: Here is the whole thing: **A preposition is a word that shows the relationship of a noun or pronoun to another word in the sentence.** Let's say that whole thing together three times.

TOGETHER (three times): **A preposition is a word that shows the relationship of a noun or pronoun to another word in the sentence.**

Instructor: I will say the list of prepositions that we have learned so far: "aboard, about, above, across, after, against, along, among, around, at." I am going to say that list for you three times. I want you to say as much of it as you can along with me.

Instructor (slowly, three times, with student joining in): Aboard, about, above, across, after, against, along, among, around, at.

Instructor: Now we will add four more prepositions to our list: "before, behind, below, beneath." Listen carefully while I say those prepositions three times. Then we will repeat them together three more times.

Instructor (three times): Before, behind, below, beneath.

TOGETHER (three times): Before, behind, below, beneath.

Instructor: Let's get up and walk around the room. First, I want you to walk before me. Where are you? You are in front of me. "Before" tells more about our relationship. Now, let's change the relationship. Walk behind me. Where are you? You aren't in front of me any more! "Behind" tells me that our relationship has changed. Now lie down on the floor.

Note to Instructor: *Stand over the student; the illustration will be clearer if you can straddle him.*

Instructor: Where are you now? Our relationship has changed again! Now you are below me. And there is also something beneath you. What is beneath you?

Student: *The floor is beneath me.*

Instructor: The preposition "beneath" tells about the relationship between you and the floor. We have learned the prepositions "before," "behind," "below," "beneath." Let's repeat those together three more times.

TOGETHER (three times): Before, behind, below, beneath.

Instructor: Now I will repeat the whole list for you, from the beginning, five times. Join in with me as far as you are able.

Instructor (slowly, five times, with student joining in): Aboard, about, above, across, after, against, along, among, around, at. Before, behind, below, beneath.

Dictation Exercise

Choose one of the following sentences. Help the student place the comma correctly.

At the library, I found many books.

Among the books, I found one about mummies.

Beneath the pyramids, mummies lie in special tombs.

Enrichment Activity

Read the phrases below one at a time and ask the student to make up the rest of the sentence.

Aboard the ship…	Around the house…
Above the ground…	At bedtime…
Across the street…	Before breakfast…
After breakfast…	Behind the bookcase…
Along the path…	Between the pages…
Among my toys…	Beneath the tree…

3/2/20

Lesson 63

·   **LESSON 63**   ·

Prepositions
Dictation exercise: "Beneath the castle wall"
Poem review: "The Goops" (Lesson 2)

Notes to Instructor: *Review "The Goops" today.*

The student may want drawing supplies for the enrichment activity.

Instructor: Today we will try to say our whole preposition definition together. Listen carefully: **A preposition is a word that shows the relationship of a noun or pronoun to another word in the sentence.** Now, let's repeat that together three times.

TOGETHER (three times): **A preposition is a word that shows the relationship of a noun or pronoun to another word in the sentence.**

Instructor: I will say the list of prepositions that we have learned so far three times. Try to say them with me.

Instructor (slowly, three times, with student joining in): Aboard, about, above, across. After, against, along, among, around, at. Before, behind, below, beneath.

Instructor: Now let's add four more prepositions to this list. I will say them for you three times.

Instructor (three times): Beside, between, beyond, by.

Instructor: Let's say those four prepositions together three times.

TOGETHER (three times): Beside, between, beyond, by.

Instructor: Let's go back and look at the picture in Lesson 60. We will practice using these prepositions as we talk about this picture. Let's find some things that are *beside*. The boats are *beside* each other. The fishermen in the boats are *beside* each other. Now, can you find something that is *between*?

Student: *The boats are between the waves.*

Note to Instructor: *If necessary, prompt the student by asking, "What are the boats between?"*

Instructor: "Beyond" means "on the other side." What is *beyond*, in the picture?

Student: *The mountain is beyond the water.*

Note to Instructor: *If necessary, prompt the student by asking, "Where is the mountain?"*

Instructor: The preposition "by" often means the same thing as "beside." It means "close to" or "near." The waves are "by" the boats.

Instructor: We have also seen "by" in another place. Let's go back and look at the poem called "Bed in Summer" (Lesson 61). Where do you see the word "by"? It tells us who wrote the poem. We often use "by" to indicate the author of a book or story or poem. It shows a relationship between a person and a poem or story. The person wrote the poem or story! That is a very important relationship. Now, let's say those four prepositions together three times more: Beside, between, beyond, by.

TOGETHER (three times): Beside, between, beyond, by.

Instructor: Now I will repeat the whole list for you, from the beginning, five times. Join in with me as far as you are able.

Instructor (slowly, five times, with student joining in): Aboard, about, above, across. After, against, along, among, around, at. Before, behind, below, beneath. Beside, between, beyond, by.

Dictation Exercise (Adapted from classic poets)

Choose one or more of the following sentences. For this lesson, dictate only these sentences. Do not dictate the author's name.

They camped beneath the castle wall.

[Adapted from "Marmion" by Sir Walter Scott]

The cold earth slept beneath the sinking moon.

[Adapted from "The Cold Earth Slept Below" by Percy Bysshe Shelley]

Beneath his sad brow, his eye flashed like a broad sword, drawn from the sheath.

[Adapted from "Excelsior!" by Henry Wadsworth Longfellow]

Enrichment Activity

Read the first stanza of "The Daffodils" together. Help the student find each preposition. Point out that "o'er" is a poetic contraction of "over." Ask the student to copy and illustrate one or more lines.

The Daffodils
By William Wordsworth

I wandered lonely as a cloud

That floats on high o'er vales and hills,

When all at once I saw a crowd,

A host, of golden daffodils;

Beside the lake, beneath the trees,

Fluttering and dancing in the breeze.

3/4/20

•   **LESSON 64**   •

Articles
Commas in a series
Conjunctions
Prepositions
Dictation exercise: "During my lesson"

Instructor: Do you remember the "little words" that we studied? The articles "a," "an," and "the" are very short words! Let's say together: **The articles are "a," "an," and "the."**

TOGETHER: **The articles are "a," "an," and "the."**

Instructor: We use "the" to talk about specific nouns. We use "a" and "an" to talk about any old noun.

Note to Instructor: *Point to a particular chair as you say the next sentence.*

Instructor: If I say "Sit in the chair," you know that you should sit in one specific chair. But if I say "Sit in a chair," you could choose any chair to sit in. Even though the articles "a" and "an" are so short, they have their own special rule. "An" comes before words that begin with vowels. Repeat after me: The vowels are a, e, i, o, u.

Student: *The vowels are a, e, i, o, u.*

Instructor: All the other letters of the alphabet are called consonants. The article "a" comes before words that begin with consonants. If I say "I will give you a gift," I use "a" before "gift" because "gift" begins with the consonant "g." If I tell you "Go get an eraser," I use "an" before "eraser" because "eraser" begins with the vowel "e." Now I am going to let you look at a tricky sentence which is almost like a word puzzle.

At the zoo, I saw an ape, an elephant, an itchy monkey, an ostrich, and an ugly baboon.

Instructor: Tell me the letters at the beginning of each animal's name.
Student: *a (ape), e (elephant), m (monkey), o (ostrich), b (baboon).*

Instructor: Now, here is the tricky part. Do the little words "a" and "an" come just before each animal's name, or are they placed just before some other word?

Note to Instructor: *Point to the article before each word. Then ask the student to name each word after the article. For "ape," "elephant," and "ostrich," remind the student that "a," "e," and "o" are vowels, and that the article "an" should come before a word that begins with a vowel. For "monkey" and "baboon," remind the student that "m" and "b" are consonants, but that "itchy" and "ugly" are the words that follow the articles and so require the article "an."*

Instructor: Look at the sentence again with me. There are five animals at the zoo. The names of the animals are all in a series or list. What punctuation mark separates the names?

Student: *A comma separates the names.*

Instructor: Remember, we use commas to separate items in a list. The last two items in this list of animals are an ostrich and an ugly baboon. Those two items are connected with the special word "and." "And" is a conjunction. Do you remember what a conjunction is?

Note to Instructor: *Prompt the student, if necessary.*

Instructor: **A conjunction joins words or groups of words together.** Let's say that together three times.

TOGETHER (three times): **A conjunction joins words or groups of words together.**

Instructor: Remember, "junction" means "joining." A road junction is a place where two roads join together. A "conjunction" in grammar is a place where two words or groups of words join together. Let's look again at the sentence about the zoo one more time. What is the very first word?

Student: *At.*

Instructor: What kind of word is "at"? You have memorized it in a list. Remember: Aboard, about, above...

Student: *"At" is a preposition.*

Instructor: **A preposition is a word that shows the relationship of a noun or pronoun to another word in the sentence.** The preposition "at" tells you about the relationship between five animals and a place. They are not in your bedroom! They are at the zoo. I will say the prepositions we have already learned for you three times. Join in with me.

Instructor (slowly, three times, with student joining in): Aboard, about, above, across. After, against, along, among, around, at. Before, behind, below, beneath. Beside, between, beyond, by.

Instructor: Now we are going to do a little march around the room, and while we march, we will say "Down, during, except, for, from!" We will say that until we are out of breath and ready to stop.

Note to Instructor: *March around the room saying "Down, during, except, for, from!" as long as seems appropriate.*

Dictation Exercise

Choose one of the following sentences. Remember to pause after the comma.

During my lesson, I worked.

During my lesson, I worked for twenty minutes.

I went down the stairs for a drink of water during a break from my lesson.

••••••••••••••••••••••• **LESSON 65** ••••••••••••••••••••••

Prepositions
Adverbs

Note to Instructor: *The student will need art supplies for the enrichment activity.*

Instructor: I will say the whole definition of a preposition for you. Then we will say it together three times. **A preposition is a word that shows the relationship of a noun or pronoun to another word in the sentence.**

TOGETHER (three times): **A preposition is a word that shows the relationship of a noun or pronoun to another word in the sentence.**

Instructor: In the last lesson, we learned five new prepositions: "down, during, except, for, from." Let's say that list together three times.

TOGETHER (three times): Down, during, except, for, from.

Instructor: Now I will say the list of prepositions we have learned so far. Say them with me three times.

TOGETHER (three times): Aboard, about, above, across. After, against, along, among, around, at. Before, behind, below, beneath. Beside, between, beyond, by. Down, during, except, for, from.

Instructor: Let's add four more prepositions to that list. I will say them for you three times.

Instructor (three times): In, inside, into, like.

Instructor: We will practice making sentences with these prepositions. I will give you two parts of a sentence, and I want you to use the preposition to show the relationship between them. The parts are "The stars twinkled" and "the sky." I will say them again: "The stars twinkled" and "the sky." Now add the preposition "in."
Student: *The stars twinkled in the sky.*

Instructor: The stars twinkled in the sky. Now I am going to add one more word: an adverb! Remember, **an adverb is a word that describes a verb, an adjective, or another adverb.** Let's repeat that together.

TOGETHER: **An adverb is a word that describes a verb, an adjective, or another adverb.**

Instructor: Now I will add the adverb "brightly." In this sentence, "The stars twinkled in the sky," my adverb will describe the verb "twinkled." Repeat this sentence after me: "The stars twinkled brightly in the sky."
Student: *The stars twinkled brightly in the sky.*

Instructor: I will give you two more sentence parts: "The sun climbed" and "the morning sky." Use the preposition "into" and show the relationship between "The sun climbed" and "the morning sky."

Note to Instructor: *For the remainder of the lesson, remember to repeat the sentence parts and the preposition until the student can remember them and repeat them back to you. This assures you that the student is listening, and also gives the student practice retaining words in his mind.*

Student: *The sun climbed into the morning sky.*

Instructor: Can you add the adverb "cheerfully" to your sentence? Remember, the adverb describes the verb "climbed."

Student: *The sun climbed cheerfully into the morning sky.*

Instructor: Put the sentence parts "The child stayed" and "the house" together using the preposition "inside."

Student: *The child stayed inside the house.*

Instructor: Now put the adverb "lazily" into your sentence. Remember, the adverb describes the verb "stayed."

Student: *The child stayed lazily inside the house.*

Instructor: Now put the sentence parts "The clouds floated in the sky" together with "whipped cream." Use the preposition "like."

Student: *The clouds floated in the sky like whipped cream.*

Instructor: Finally, add the adverb "gently" to your sentence. Remember, the adverb describes the verb "floated."

Student: *The clouds floated gently in the sky like whipped cream.*

Instructor: Repeat with me three times: "in, inside, into, like."

Together (three times): In, inside, into, like.

Instructor: I will say the whole list of prepositions three times. See if you can say them along with me.

Instructor (slowly, three times, with student joining in): Aboard, about, above, across. After, against, along, among, around, at. Before, behind, below, beneath. Beside, between, beyond, by. Down, during, except, for, from. In, inside, into, like.

Enrichment Activity

Ask the student to draw a picture of the scene described in the lesson. Include the cheerful sun, the house, the student resting in the house, and the whipped-cream clouds. He could paste cotton in the sky if he wishes. You may wish to use the picture to review the relationships described in the lesson.

· **LESSON 66** · · · · · · · · · · · · · · · · · ·   3/11/20

Prepositions
Verbs

Instructor: In our last lesson, we learned the prepositions "in," "inside," "into," "like." Say those for me.

Student: *In, inside, into, like.*

Instructor: I will say the whole long list of prepositions three times. I want you to see if you can say all of them with me!

Instructor (slowly, three times, with student joining in): Aboard, about, above, across. After, against, along, among, around, at. Before, behind, below, beneath. Beside, between, beyond, by. Down, during, except, for, from. In, inside, into, like.

Instructor: Now let's read a new poem together. I will read it as you follow along.

I Love You Well
Mother Goose rhyme

I love you well, my little brother,

And you are fond of me;

Let us be kind to one another,

As brothers ought to be.

You shall learn to play with me,

And learn to use my toys;

And then I think that we shall be

Two happy little boys.

Instructor: Together, we will find the different kinds of verbs in this poem. I will remind you of the definition of a verb. **A verb is a word that does an action, shows a state of being, links two words together, or helps another verb**. Let's say that together three times.

155

TOGETHER (three times): **A verb is a word that does an action, shows a state of being, links two words together, or helps another verb.**

Instructor: Can we find action verbs in this poem? Remember, action verbs tell about something that you can do.

   Note to Instructor: *The action verbs in the poem are "love" (first line), "learn" (fifth line), "play" (fifth line), "learn" (sixth line), "use" (sixth line), and "think" (seventh line).*

Instructor: The second part of your definition is "A verb shows a state of being." Remember, the state of being verbs show that someone exists. Here is the list of state of being verbs: Am, is, are, was, were, be, being, been. Let's chant those together three times.

TOGETHER (three times): Am, is, are, was, were, be, being, been.

Instructor: Remember sentences with state of being verbs can be very short: "I was," or "He was." Another kind of verb called a linking verb connects a noun or pronoun with another word. There is a linking verb in the second line of this poem: "And you are fond of me." The verb "are" links "you" to "fond." "Fond" tells us a little bit more about the little brother in the poem. He likes his older brother! "Are" is the linking verb. Let's look at the poem again.

I Love You Well
Mother Goose rhyme

I love you well, my little brother,

And you are fond of me;

Let us be kind to one another,

As brothers ought to be.

You shall learn to play with me,

And learn to use my toys;

And then I think that we shall be

Two happy little boys.

Instructor: Now look at the last two lines of the poem: "And then I think that we shall be/Two happy little boys." There are two words between "we" and "two happy little boys." They link "we" and "two happy little boys." What are those two words?

Student: *Shall be.*

Instructor: "Be" is a linking verb. It links "we" to the words that give more information about the little boys. They are happy! "Shall" is a helping verb. Remember, some verbs help other verbs. "Shall" is helping the linking verb "be." Can you find another place in the poem where "shall" helps a verb?

Student: *Shall learn.*

Instructor: Good! I will say the list of helping verbs for you.
Am [clap]
Is [clap]
Are, was, were [clap]
Be [clap]
Being [clap]
Been [clap] [clap]
Have, has, had [clap]
Do, does, did [clap]
Shall, will, should, would, may, might, must [clap] [clap]
Can, could!

Instructor: Let's say that together three times.

TOGETHER (three times):
Am [clap]
Is [clap]
Are, was, were [clap]
Be [clap]
Being [clap]
Been [clap] [clap]
Have, has, had [clap]
Do, does, did [clap]
Shall, will, should, would, may, might, must [clap] [clap]
Can, could!

Enrichment Activity

Have the student work on memorizing the poem "I Love You Well."

••••••••••••••••••••••   **LESSON 67**   ••••••••••••••••••••

Prepositions
Dictation exercise: "King of the stuffed animals"
Poem review: "The Little Bird" (Lesson 39)

Notes to Instructor: *Prepare for today's lesson by setting a chair in the middle of the room. This will be a "throne." You may throw a blanket over it or put a special cushion on it if you wish.*

The student will need art supplies for the enrichment activity.

Review "The Little Bird" today.

Instructor:	Go and get me one of your favorite stuffed animals. He will help us learn our new prepositions today! Today, he has been appointed "King of the Stuffed Animals." Set him on his throne! The king is on the throne. What is the relationship between the king and the throne?
Student:	*The king is on the throne.*
Instructor:	"On" is a preposition that tells us more about the relationship between the king and his throne. Oh! I hear a fierce growl outside the door! The lion, who is king of the jungle, isn't sure he likes the Stuffed Animal King. I think your king had better get off his throne! Set him on the floor, where he can pretend that he isn't really the king. He is off the throne. Now, what is the relationship between the king and his throne?
Student:	*The king is off his throne.*
Instructor:	He is off his throne, but he is still near it. "Off" and "near" are both prepositions that tell us more about the relationship between the king and his throne. He is off it, but he is still near it. Oh, dear, I hear the lion again! Perhaps the king should hide under his throne. Now his throne is over him! "Over" is also a preposition. The king has had many different kinds of relationships with his throne! He has been on the throne, off the throne, and near the throne. Now the throne is over him!

Note to Instructor: *You may pause at this point and allow the student to create other relationships between the King and his throne: under, behind, below, beneath, above.*

Instructor:	There is one more preposition that we need to know today. It is the preposition "of." Your stuffed animal is the King of the Stuffed Animals. "Of" describes the relationship between the king and the stuffed animals! "Of" is a very useful preposition. The king's throne is made of wood [or metal]. "Of" tells about the relationship between the wood (or metal) and the chair. If the king had a crown, it might be made of gold. "Of" tells about the relationship between the crown and the gold. Do you remember the definition of a preposition? **A preposition is a word that shows the relationship of a noun**

or pronoun to another word in the sentence. We have talked about many different relationships today! Now say that definition together with me three times.

TOGETHER (three times): **A preposition is a word that shows the relationship of a noun or pronoun to another word in the sentence.**

Instructor: Let's repeat the prepositions that we used today three times: near, of, off, on, over.

TOGETHER (three times): Near, of, off, on, over.

Instructor: Now listen to the entire list of prepositions that we have learned so far: "aboard, about, above, across. After, against, along, among, around, at. Before, behind, below, beneath. Beside, between, beyond, by. Down, during, except, for, from. In, inside, into, like. Near, of, off, on, over." I will say that whole list three times, and I want you to try to say it along with me.

Instructor (slowly, three times, with student joining in): Aboard, about, above, across. After, against, along, among, around, at. Before, behind, below, beneath. Beside, between, beyond, by. Down, during, except, for, from. In, inside, into, like. Near, of, off, on, over.

Dictation Exercise

Choose one of the following sentences to dictate. Pause at the comma.

[Stuffed animal's name] is king of the stuffed animals.

He sits on his throne and rules over them.

But when the lion is near, [stuffed animal's name] jumps off his throne.

Enrichment Activity

Make the King of the Stuffed Animals a crown of gold paper. Point out that "of" expresses the relationship between the crown and the gold paper.

3/20/20

• **LESSON 68** •

Prepositions
Dictation exercise: "Through the rain"

Instructor: Listen while I recite the entire list of prepositions that we have learned so far: "Aboard, about, above, across. After, against, along, among, around, at. Before, behind, below, beneath. Beside, between, beyond, by. Down, during, except, for, from. In, inside, into, like. Near, of, off, on, over." I will say that whole list three times, and I want you to try to say it along with me.

Instructor (slowly, three times, with student joining in): Aboard, about, above, across. After, against, along, among, around, at. Before, behind, below, beneath. Beside, between, beyond, by. Down, during, except, for, from. In, inside, into, like. Near, of, off, on, over.

Instructor: Today, we are learning four very interesting, new prepositions. The first preposition is "past." Let's take a little walk around the house together, and talk about the things that we walk past.

Note to Instructor: *You can also walk around the yard, if you prefer. Each time you pass something that can be named, say "We just walked past the door." "We just walked past the sofa." "We just walked past your bed." Continue walking and talking until you are ready to return to the lesson area.*

Instructor: The preposition "past" tells about the relationship between you and an object you leave behind you. Once you leave it, it is "past" you. The next preposition on today's list is "since." This word tells us about time. Repeat these sentences after me: "I have not eaten breakfast since this morning."

Student: *I have not eaten breakfast since this morning.*

Instructor: I have not taken a bath since yesterday.
Student: *I have not taken a bath since yesterday.*

Instructor: We have been talking about prepositions since Lesson 58!
Student: *We have been talking about prepositions since Lesson 58!*

Note to Instructor: *"Since" also acts as an adverb and as a conjunction. Distinguishing between the uses of "since" is too complicated for a young student. Do not ask the student to make up sentences with "since"; most children will naturally use it as an adverb or conjunction, rather than a preposition. (See a dictionary for examples of each usage.)*

Instructor: The next preposition is "through." Let's take another little walk through the kitchen. We will start on one side of the kitchen and go all the way through the kitchen to the other side. "Through" means "from one side to the other." We go through tunnels and doors. No one wants to stay in a tunnel or a door! You go from one side of it to the other—and out! The last preposition is "throughout." If I say "It rained throughout the day," did the rain ever stop?

Student: *No.*

Instructor: "We searched for the library book throughout the house." Did we search the whole house?

Student: *Yes.*

Instructor: We searched the house from top to bottom! "Throughout" is another way of saying "the whole thing, from beginning to end." Now I will say our four new prepositions three times.

Instructor (three times): Past, since, through, throughout.

Instructor: Say those prepositions with me three times.

Together (three times): Past, since, through, throughout.

Instructor: I am going to write these prepositions for you to see.

> **Note to Instructor:** *Let the student watch as you print the four new prepositions (past, since, through, throughout).*

Instructor: Now, I am going to read some sentences and play a trick on you. When I get to one of these prepositions, I am going to say the word "preposition" instead! I want you to decide which new preposition would fit in that place. Then you repeat the sentence back to me and say a real preposition.

> Note to Instructor: *You may need to repeat each sentence more than once.*

Instructor: I always walk slowly when I walk [preposition] the toy store window.
Student: *I always walk slowly when I walk <u>past</u> the toy store window.*

Instructor: When Grandma burned the supper, the smoke spread [preposition] the house.
Student: *When Grandma burned the supper, the smoke spread <u>throughout</u> the house.*

> **Note to Instructor:** *If the student uses the preposition "through," ask, "Did the smoke fill the house, or did it just go in one door and out another?"*

Instructor: I have grown an inch [preposition] last year.
Student: *I have grown an inch <u>since</u> last year.*

Instructor: The children playing cops and robbers ran screaming [preposition] the house.
Student: *The children playing cops and robbers ran screaming <u>through</u> the house.*

Instructor: Let's say "past, since, through, throughout" together three more times.

TOGETHER (three times): Past, since, through, throughout.

Dictation Exercise (Adapted from classic poets)

Choose one of the following sentences. Do not dictate the author's name.

I see the lights gleam through the rain and mist.

[From "The Day is Done" by Phoebe Cary]

Sound the trumpet, beat the drum, throughout all the world around.

[From "The Secular Masque" by John Dryden]

Wild winter wind, storm throughout the night, and dash the black clouds against the sky.

[From "Safe" by Augusta Webster]

· · · · · · · · · · · · · · · · · · · **LESSON 69** · · · · · · · · · · · · · · · · · · ·

Cumulative poem review   3/24/20

Note to Instructor: *Review all poems memorized up to this point.*

Lesson	Poem	Author
2	"The Goops"	Gelett Burgess
31	"The Year"	Sara Coleridge, adapted by Sara Buffington
39	"The Little Bird"	Mother Goose rhyme
51	"The Months"	Mother Goose rhyme

Note to Instructor: *You may also read back through the poems that were not memorized.*

"The Wind"	Lesson 15
"Against Quarrelling and Fighting"	Lesson 26
"How Creatures Move"	Lesson 29
"Whole Duty of Children"	Lesson 48
"Days of the Week"	Lesson 51
"Bed in Summer" (one stanza)	Lesson 61
"The Daffodils" (one stanza)	Lesson 63
"I Love You Well"	Lesson 66

• **LESSON 70** •

3|24|20

Letter writing: Writing a friendly letter
Prepositions
Copywork: Writing a letter

Instructor: Today, we are going to work on a letter to a friend. But first, we need to review our preposition list! I will say it for you once, and then we will try to say it together three more times. "Aboard, about, above, across. After, against, along, among, around, at. Before, behind, below, beneath. Beside, between, beyond, by. Down, during, except, for, from. In, inside, into, like. Near, of, off, on, over. Past, since, through, throughout."

Instructor (slowly, three times, with student joining in): Aboard, about, above, across. After, against, along, among, around, at. Before, behind, below, beneath. Beside, between, beyond, by. Down, during, except, for, from. In, inside, into, like. Near, of, off, on, over. Past, since, through, throughout.

Instructor: After we write our letter, we will send it to a friend. Can you guess what kind of word "to" might be?

Note to Instructor: *If necessary, prompt student by saying: What is the relationship between your letter and the friend?*

Instructor: "To" is a preposition. It tells us more about the relationship between the letter and your friend. Your friend will receive the letter. "Toward" is also a preposition. You will send the letter to your friend, and it will move toward him through the mail. Answer me in a complete sentence. To whom will you send your letter?

Note to Instructor: *The student will write a friendly letter in this lesson. Help him decide on a recipient. Then ask the student to put this name into a complete sentence.*

Student: *I will send my letter to [name of friend].*

Instructor: The other prepositions we will add to our list are the prepositions "under" and "underneath." Both words mean the same thing. Do you remember when the king of the stuffed animals hid under his throne? We could also say "He hid underneath his throne," and it would mean the same thing. Listen to me say those four prepositions three times, and then we will say them three times together.

Instructor (three times): To, toward, under, underneath.

TOGETHER (three times): To, toward, under, underneath.

Instructor: Now let's work on our letter to [name of friend]. You will tell me what you want to say to your friend, and I will write the letter out for you. Then you will copy part of the letter

164

onto your own paper. You will finish copying the letter tomorrow.

Note to Instructor. *Make suggestions about content: tell about a school project, a model the student has recently made, a science observation, an interesting person or fact from history, or a recent family activity. Write the letter out for the student, following the form below. Aim for four or five sentences in the body of the letter. Indent the first line of the paragraph and simply explain to the student that the first line of the letter should begin about the width of two fingers from the margin.*

Date (Today's date, written on the right-hand side of the paper)

Greeting (Dear _____,)
(Remember that a comma comes after the greeting. Remind the student that a title of respect which is abbreviated begins with a capital letter and has a period following it).

Body of the Letter (This week, we went to see a play...)

Closing (You may use "Love," "Sincerely," or "Yours truly." Remember that a comma comes after the closing. The closing should be in line with the date above.)

Writer's Name (Student signs his own name.)

Copywork

Ask the student to copy the first half of his letter. If the letter is too long for the student to copy comfortably, finish writing the first half for him.

• • • • • • • • • • • • • • • • • • **LESSON 71** • • • • • • • • • • • • • • • • • •

3/25/20

Addressing an envelope

Note to Instructor: *The student will need a business-size envelope and a first-class stamp.*

Instructor: Before we continue copying our letter, let's review our preposition list. I will say it for you once, and then we will try to say it together three more times. "Aboard, about, above, across. After, against, along, among, around, at. Before, behind, below, beneath. Beside, between, beyond, by. Down, during, except, for, from. In, inside, into, like. Near, of, off, on, over. Past, since, through, throughout. To, toward, under, underneath."

Instructor (slowly, three times, with student joining in): Aboard, about, above, across. After, against, along, among, around, at. Before, behind, below, beneath. Beside, between, beyond, by. Down, during, except, for, from. In, inside, into, like. Near, of, off, on, over. Past, since, through, throughout. To, toward, under, underneath.

Instructor: Repeat after me: **A preposition is a word that shows the relationship of a noun or pronoun to another word in the sentence.**

Student: *A preposition is a word that shows the relationship of a noun or pronoun to another word in the sentence.*

Instructor: Today, I want you to finish copying out your letter, as neatly as you can.

Note to Instructor: *Give the student time to complete his copying of the letter. If the letter is too long for him to copy comfortably, you may finish it for him.*

Instructor: Now, I will write your name and address on a piece of paper. You will copy this name and address into the left-hand corner of an envelope. I will also write the name and address of your friend. You will copy this name and address in the center of the envelope.

Note to Instructor: *Draw light lines on the envelope, as illustrated on the next page, to help guide the student's writing. As he writes, point out the abbreviations. Remind him that a ZIP code helps the post office send the envelope to the right place. Remind him to use a period after titles of respect and other appropriate abbreviations.*

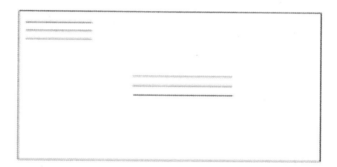

When the student is finished copying the letter and the envelope, help him fold the letter neatly, put it in the envelope, and mail it. Remember that letters this size should be folded into thirds. First, fold up the bottom third, and then fold down the top third. If he has difficulty copying the address, you may help him.

·   **LESSON 72**   · · · · · · · · · · · · · · · · · · ·

Prepositions

Instructor: Today, we are going to learn the very last of the prepositions! First, let's review the prepositions we have already learned. I will say them for you once, and then we will try to say them together three more times. "Aboard, about, above, across. After, against, along, among, around, at. Before, behind, below, beneath. Beside, between, beyond, by. Down, during, except, for, from. In, inside, into, like. Near, of, off, on, over. Past, since, through, throughout. To, toward, under, underneath."

Instructor (slowly, three times, with student joining in): Aboard, about, above, across. After, against, along, among, around, at. Before, behind, below, beneath. Beside, between, beyond, by. Down, during, except, for, from. In, inside, into, like. Near, of, off, on, over. Past, since, through, throughout. To, toward, under, underneath.

Instructor: We are going to add the last prepositions to this list. I will say these last six prepositions for you three times, and then we will say them three more times together.

Instructor (three times): Until, up, upon. With, within, without.

Together (three times): Until, up, upon. With, within, without.

Instructor: "Until" means "Up to the time of." If we read until lights out time, we read up to the time of lights out. If we swim until five o'clock, we swim up to the time of five o'clock. Put the preposition "until" together with the phrases "We will do our school" and "lunch."

Student: *We will do our school until lunch.*

Instructor: "Up" is an easy preposition. If I tell you "Climb up the stairs," will you know what to do? What if I tell you that the eensy-weensy spider went up the waterspout? Do you know what the spider is doing? "Upon" is another easy preposition. It has the same meaning as "on." "Put the plate upon the table" means the same thing as "Put the plate on the table." I will give you two sentences with "on" in them. Replace the preposition "on" with the preposition "upon." "Put your shoes on your feet.

Student: *Put your shoes upon your feet.*

Instructor: Put your hands on your head.

Student: *Put your hands upon your head.*

Instructor: Now you have learned the prepositions "until," "up," "upon." The preposition "with" means "together." Do you like ice cream with hot fudge sauce?

Student: *Yes!*

Instructor: Finish the following sentences for me: "I like to play with…"

Student:	*I like to play with [toys, my friends, my brother].*
Instructor:	I prefer to eat my hot dogs with…
Student:	*I prefer to eat my hot dogs with [mustard].*

Instructor: "Within" is the next preposition. It means "inside." If I tell you that you will find great wisdom within your grammar book, it means that wisdom is inside your grammar book! If I say "We will be finished with this lesson within the hour," it means that we are only doing grammar during this hour. It will not go over into the next hour! Put these two phrases together for me, using the preposition "within": "It is thundering, so stay" and "the house."

Student: *It is thundering, so stay within the house.*

Instructor: And now we have reached our very last preposition! "Without" means that you do not have something. If I tell you "Sleep in your room without a light," do you have a light?

Student: *No, I do not have a light.*

Instructor: If you ask to buy an expensive toy, and I say "No, you will have to do without the toy!" are you going to get the toy?

Student: *No, I will not get the toy.*

Instructor: If I say "You have done all of your work without complaint!" have you complained today?

Student: *No, I have not complained.*

Instructor: Now, I will say those last six prepositions again: "Until, up, upon. With, within, without." Say them with me three more times.

TOGETHER (three times): Until, up, upon. With, within, without.

Instructor: Now it is time to do the whole list! I will say them for you once, and then we will try to say them together three more times. "Aboard, about, above, across. After, against, along, among, around, at. Before, behind, below, beneath. Beside, between, beyond, by. Down, during, except, for, from. In, inside, into, like. Near, of, off, on, over. Past, since, through, throughout. To, toward, under, underneath. Until, up, upon. With, within, without."

Instructor (slowly, three times, with student joining in): Aboard, about, above, across. After, against, along, among, around, at. Before, behind, below, beneath. Beside, between, beyond, by. Down, during, except, for, from. In, inside, into, like. Near, of, off, on, over. Past, since, through, throughout. To, toward, under, underneath. Until, up, upon. With, within, without.

Instructor: I will read the following poem to you. Follow along with me as I read.

3/26/20

Foreign Lands

By Robert Louis Stevenson

Up into the cherry tree

Who should climb but little me?

I held the trunk with both my hands

And looked abroad on foreign lands.

I saw the next door garden lie,

Adorned with flowers, before my eye,

And many pleasant places more

That I had never seen before.

I saw the dimpling river pass

And be the sky's blue looking-glass;

The dusty roads go up and down

With people tramping into town.

If I could find a higher tree

Farther and farther I should see,

To where the grown-up river slips

Into the sea among the ships,

To where the roads on either hand

Lead onward into fairy land,

Where all the children dine at five,

And all the playthings come alive.

Instructor: I will point out some prepositions in the poem "Foreign Lands." Each preposition shows a relationship between two words. I am going to ask you to tell me which two words are related. In the third line, "I held the trunk with both my hands," the preposition "with" shows a relationship between what two words?

Note to Instructor: *If the student cannot answer, read the line again, emphasizing the words in bold print: "I held the* **trunk** *with both my* **hands."**

Student: "Trunk" and "hands." ["both" is also acceptable].

Instructor: In the third stanza, the student in the tree sees "people tramping into town." The preposition "into" shows a relationship between what two words?

Note to Instructor: *If necessary, read the line again: "People tramping into town."*

Student: "People" and "town."

Instructor: In the fourth stanza, the student sees that the "river slips into the sea." The preposition "into" shows a relationship between what two words?

Note to Instructor: *If necessary, read the line again: "River slips into the sea."*

Student: "River" and "sea."

·   **LESSON 73**   ·

3/31/20

Story narration: "The Three Bears"

Note to Instructor: *Read aloud the story below. Then ask the "starter questions" at the end of the story. Remember to encourage the student to answer in complete sentences. Then ask the student, "What is one thing you remember form the story?" Write his answer down and read it back to him.*

The Three Bears
Retold by Sara Buffington

Once upon a time there were three bears who lived together in a charming cottage in the woods. They were Great Big Papa Bear, Medium-sized Mama Bear, and Itty-bitty Baby Bear. They had just fixed their breakfast of porridge, but it was too hot to eat. So they decided to take a walk in the woods. They hoped that the porridge would be cool enough to eat when they got home. So they opened the charming blue door of their charming wood cottage, walked down their charming walkway lined with charming red roses, and left.

While the bears were off on their woodland walk, a little girl named Goldilocks happened by the cottage. She was a pretty girl, named for her long, golden locks of hair, but she was also very naughty. So when she saw the charming cottage of the bear family, she said to herself, "Oh! That is the most charming wood cottage with the most charming red roses and the most charming blue door. I must go inside and look around." It never occurred to her to ask for permission or to knock on the door. As I already explained, she was a naughty, rude little girl.

Inside she found three bowls of porridge: one big, one medium-sized, and one very small. She tasted the porridge in the big, blue bowl.

"Ow!" she cried out. "That porridge is too hot!"

Then she tasted the porridge in the medium-sized, red bowl. "Yuck!" she whined. "That porridge is too cold!"

Then she tasted the very small, yellow bowl of porridge. "Mmm!" she exclaimed. "This porridge is neither too hot nor too cold. This is just right." And she gobbled up the whole bowl.

Now, she was very full from eating the porridge, so she decided to take a rest.

Near the fireplace, she saw three rocking chairs: one big, one medium-sized, and one very small. First she sat in the big rocking chair. It had a big, blue cushion on it.

"Oh!" she complained. "That cushion is too hard!" So she jumped off the rocking chair and threw the big, blue cushion on the floor. Then she sat in the medium-sized rocking chair. It had a medium-sized, red cushion on it.

"Hmph!" she grumbled. "That cushion is too soft!" So she jumped off the rocking chair and threw the medium-sized, red cushion on the floor.

Then she sat in the very small rocking chair. It had a very small, yellow cushion on it. "Ah!" she sighed. "This cushion is neither too hard nor too soft. This cushion is just right." So she rocked and she rocked and she rocked until she broke the very small rocking chair!

She was very tired from all that rocking, so she climbed up the stairs to the bedroom. There she found three beds: one big, one medium-sized, and one very small. First she lay down in the big bed with the blue blanket.

"Ooh!" she groaned. "That blanket is too thick!" So she tossed the blanket aside and hopped out of bed. Then she lay down in the medium-sized bed with the red blanket on it.

"Brrr," she shivered. "That blanket is too thin!" So she tossed that blanket aside and hopped out of bed.

Then she lay down in the very small bed with the yellow blanket on it. "Mmm," she murmured. "This blanket is neither too thick nor too thin. This blanket is just right." And she fell fast asleep.

Just then the bear family came back from their walk. Great Big Papa Bear lumbered over to his porridge bowl. He bellowed in his big, gruff, booming voice:

"Somebody has been eating my porridge!"

Medium-sized Mama Bear padded over to her porridge bowl. She exclaimed in her medium-sized, surprised voice:

"Somebody has been eating my porridge!"

Then Itty-bitty Baby Bear scampered over to his porridge bowl. He cried in his high, shrill, squeaky voice:

"Somebody has been eating my porridge, and has eaten every last drop!"

Then the Bear family went over to the rocking chairs. They needed to sit down to recover from the shock of their porridge having been eaten. Great Big Papa Bear saw his big, blue cushion lying on the floor. He boomed in his great, big voice:

"Somebody has been sitting in my chair!"

Then Medium-sized Mama Bear noticed her medium-sized, red cushion lying on the floor. She cried out in her medium-sized voice:

"Somebody has been sitting in my chair!"

Then Itty-bitty Baby Bear saw his broken rocking chair. He squealed in his very small, but very high-pitched, voice:

"Someone has been sitting in my chair, and has broken the leg off!"

The bears were so upset that they decided they had better go lie down for a rest. Itty-bitty Baby Bear was the most upset, and he cried all the way up the stairs. When they got to the bedroom, Great Big Papa Bear saw his blue blanket crumpled at the end of his big bed. He thundered:

"Somebody has been sleeping in my bed!"

Then Medium-sized Mama Bear saw her red blanket hanging off the end of her medium-sized bed. She exclaimed in her medium-sized voice:

"Somebody has been sleeping in my bed!"

Then Itty-bitty Baby Bear saw that his bed linens were rumpled, too. And there, on the pillow, sleeping deeply, lay Goldilocks. Itty-bitty Baby Bear (who was already quite upset, as you can imagine) cried out in his high, squeaky, piercing voice:

"Somebody has been sleeping in my bed, and she is still in it!"

Upon hearing Itty-bitty Baby Bear's shrill voice, Goldilocks bolted wide awake. There she saw a most terrifying sight: a whole bear family leaning over her bed and looking very annoyed! She let out a little scream, dashed out of bed, flew down the stairs and out of the charming wood cottage with the charming blue door. The bears never saw her again.

The bears, exhausted by the whole experience, lay down for a long nap. What else was there to do about the matter? And just as they had thought, when they awoke they felt a lot better. As for Goldilocks, I don't know what happened to her afterwards. But I feel sure that the next time she saw a charming cottage, she went right past it, walking on her merry way.

Note to Instructor: *Ask the student to tell you the story back in his own words. If the student has trouble remembering, use these questions:*

Instructor: Who lived in the cottage?
Student: *The three bears lived in the cottage.*

Instructor: Where did they go?
Student: *They went for a walk in the woods.*

Instructor: What happened while they were gone?
Student: *Goldilocks went into their cottage.*

Instructor: What did Goldilocks do first?
Student: *She ate the porridge.*

Instructor: After she ate the porridge, what did she do?
Student: *She rocked in the rocking chairs.*

Instructor: What happened to Itty-bitty Baby Bear's chair?
Student: *She broke it.*

Instructor: After she rocked in the chairs, what did she do?
Student: *She lay down in the beds.*

Instructor: When the bears came home, how did they react to seeing their porridge eaten and their chair cushions on the floor?
Student: *They were very upset.*

Instructor: Which bear was the most upset?
Student: *Baby Bear was the most upset.*

Instructor: Where did the bears find Goldilocks?
Student: *She was sleeping in Baby Bear's bed.*

Instructor: What did Goldilocks do when she saw the bears?
Student: *She ran out of the house.*

Instructor: What did the bears do after Goldilocks left?
Student: *They took a nap.*

······· **LESSON 74** ·······

Introducing synonyms
Dictation exercise: "Roller coasters"

Note to Instructor: *Chant the preposition list twice today (this should take about ninety seconds): Aboard, about, above, across. After, against, along, among, around, at. Before, behind, below, beneath. Beside, between, beyond, by. Down, during, except, for, from. In, inside, into, like. Near, of, off, on, over. Past, since, through, throughout. To, toward, under, underneath. Until, up, upon. With, within, without.*

Instructor: Today we are going to learn about a fun kind of word: synonyms! Synonyms are words that mean the same thing. I'm going to read you part of the story "The Three Bears" again. Listen to the words that I emphasize.

Note to Instructor: *Emphasize the words in bold print.*

Goldilocks tasted the porridge in the big, blue bowl.

"Ow!" she cried out. "That porridge is too hot!"

Then she tasted the porridge in the medium-sized, red bowl. "Yuck!" she **whined**. "That is too cold!"

She sat in the big rocking chair. It had a big, blue cushion on it.

"Oh!" she **complained**. "That cushion is too hard!" So she jumped off the rocking chair and threw the big, blue cushion on the floor. Then she sat in the medium-sized rocking chair. It had a medium-sized, red cushion on it.

"Hmph!" she **grumbled**. "That cushion is too soft!" So she jumped off the rocking chair and threw the medium-sized, red cushion on the floor.

Instructor: When Goldilocks didn't like the porridge and the chairs at the house of The Three Bears, she complained, whined, and grumbled. Those three words all have the same meaning. They are synonyms. **Synonyms are words that have the same meaning.** Listen to me repeat that definition, and then we will say it together three times: **Synonyms are words that have the same meaning.**

TOGETHER (three times): **Synonyms are words that have the same meaning.**

Instructor: You can remember that synonyms have the same meaning by thinking to yourself: "SSSSynonyms have the sssssame meaning." We will read several lists of synonyms together. For each list, I will give you a sentence. I want you to say the sentence back to me three times, each time choosing a different synonym. I will do the first one for you. Here is the list of synonyms.

happy

glad

joyful

pleased

delighted

Instructor: Here is the sentence.

The father was *happy* to see his son.

> You would say back to me: "The father was glad to see his son. The father was pleased to see his son. The father was delighted to see his son." Now let's read the second list of synonyms together.

cold

chilly

freezing

icy

frosty

wintry

Instructor: Here is the sentence.

In January, the nights are *cold*.

Note to Instructor: *Allow the student to look at the list of synonyms while repeating this sentence three times, substituting a different synonym for "cold" each time. Follow the same procedure for the following lists and sentences.*

Roller coasters are so exciting that they make me shout!

shout, yell, shriek, scream, screech, squeal, holler, whoop

The traveller gazed in amazement at the big mountain.

big, large, grand, majestic, huge, immense, colossal, gigantic

I am so late that I must run home.

run, sprint, jog, dash, speed, dart, zip, hasten

I should not talk when my mother is talking to me!

talk, chatter, speak, converse, prattle

Dictation Exercise

Choose one of the sentences above. Read it to the student twice, each time using a different synonym. Let the student choose the synonyms he would like to hear. Then you dictate one of the sentences for him to write from memory.

4/6/20

·   **LESSON 75**   · · · · · · · · · · · · · · · · · · ·

Introducing antonyms
Dictation exercise: "Brush your teeth"

Notes to Instructor: The student will need art supplies for the enrichment activity.

Chant the preposition list twice today (this should take about ninety seconds): Aboard, about, above, across. After, against, along, among, around, at. Before, behind, below, beneath. Beside, between, beyond, by. Down, during, except, for, from. In, inside, into, like. Near, of, off, on, over. Past, since, through, throughout. To, toward, under, underneath. Until, up, upon. With, within, without.

Instructor: In the last lesson, we learned the definition of a synonym. Listen to me repeat that definition, and then we will say it together three times. **Synonyms are words that have the same meaning.**

TOGETHER (three times): **Synonyms are words that have the same meaning.**

Instructor: Remember, "SSSSynonyms have the ssssame meaning." **Antonyms are opposites.** Let's say that together three times: **Antonyms are opposites.**

TOGETHER (three times): **Antonyms are opposites.**

Instructor: Now I want you to do the opposite of everything I say. Stand up! What are you doing?

    Note to Instructor: *If necessary, prompt the student to do the action indicated in the student's dialogue below.*

Student: *I am sitting down.*

Instructor: Smile! What are you doing?
Student: *I am frowning.*

Instructor: Laugh! What are you doing?
Student: *I am crying.*

Instructor: Wake up! What are you doing?
Student: *I am sleeping.*

Instructor: Now we will play a game called "Contradictions." You have been contradicting. "Contradiction" is when you say the opposite of what someone says to you. I will say a sentence, and I want you to say the sentence back to me—with an opposite meaning. For example, if I say to you, "I am so happy!" I want you to say "I am so sad!" Here is the first sentence: "That cat is so fat!"

Note to Instructor: *If necessary, prompt the student to substitute the antonym given. However, the suggested dialogue for the student is only one option—if the student chooses another word of opposite meaning, accept it.*

Student:	*That cat is so thin!*

Instructor:	The glass is certainly full.
Student:	*The glass is certainly empty.*

Instructor:	It is cold in here!
Student:	*It is hot in here.*

Instructor:	I like my food raw.
Student:	*I like my food cooked* or *I hate my food raw.*

Instructor:	Time to work!
Student:	*Time to play!*

Instructor:	This chair is too hard!
Student:	*This chair is too soft!*

Instructor:	Go out!
Student:	*Come in!*

Instructor:	You just used two antonyms. "Come" is the opposite of "go." "In" is the opposite of "out." That was very good!

Note to Instructor: *Wait to see if the student offers: That was very bad. If not, repeat "That was very good!" several times with emphasis, until he contradicts you.*

Dictation Exercise

Choose one of the following sentences. Remember to pause at commas.

Brush your teeth up and down.

I have a little shadow that goes in and out with me.

When she was good, she was very, very, good, but when she was bad, she was horrid.

Enrichment Activity

Ask the student to draw pictures illustrating the following pairs of antonyms:

fat/thin

happy/sad

wide/narrow

tall/short

in/out

up/down

•••••••••••••••••••   **LESSON 76**   ••••••••••••••••••

Picture narration: "Snowy owls," by John James Audubon

Instructor: Look at the picture while I tell you about the artist, John James Audubon. He was French, but he was born in Haiti over two hundred years ago. He came to live in the United States of America when he was eighteen years old. He wanted to draw birds that were realistic and looked exactly like birds in nature, so he spent years studying them and learning about their habits. He painted seven hundred different kinds of birds and published the paintings in a book called *Birds of America*.

What pattern is on the back of the snowy owl? You can see it on the bottom owl.

Student: *The owl's back is barred.*

Instructor: What color is the snowy owl's chest? You can see it on the top owl.

Student: *The owl's chest is white.*

Instructor: What does the sky look like?

Student: *The sky is cloudy.*

Instructor: What is on the trunk of the tree?

Student: *There is bark on the trunk.*

Note to Instructor: *If necessary, prompt the student for this answer.*

Instructor: Can you see the owls' claws? Why or why not?

Student: *I can't see the owls' claws because there are feathers over them.*

Instructor: What are the owls perched on?

Student: *They are perched on a dead tree.*

Instructor: The owls are sitting on the tree's limbs. Do you know what a synonym for "limb" is? "Branch" is a synonym for "limb." We can also say that the owls are sitting on the tree's branches and it would mean the same thing.

Instructor: Which one of the owls is looking at you?

Student: *The bottom owl is looking at me.*

Instructor: Which one of the owls is smaller?

Student: *The top owl is smaller.*

Note to Instructor: *You can view this painting at the National Museum of Wildlife Art website. Go to http://www.wildlifeart.org/ViewArtwork/index.php?tID=481 or search http://www.wildlifeart.org/search for "snowy owls."*

Four types of sentences
Poem review: "The Year" (Lesson 31)

Note to Instructor: *Review "The Year" today.*

Instructor: Do you remember what a sentence is? I will help you begin: A sentence is a group...
Student: A sentence is a group of words that expresses a complete thought.

Note to Instructor: *If the student cannot complete the definition, tell him the definition and ask him to repeat it with you three times.*

Instructor: There are four types of sentences. The first type of sentence is a statement. **A statement gives information.** Statements end with periods. Let's imagine that you have a very hungry, friendly baby puppy outside! The puppy whined and barked because it was so hungry, so you went out and took care of it. What did you do for the puppy?
Student: *I fed the puppy.*

Instructor: "I fed the puppy" is a statement. It gives information. The second type of sentence is a command. **A command gives an order or makes a request.** Commands usually end with a period. If you and I heard a hungry, friendly, imaginary baby puppy howling and barking at our door, what command might I give you so that you would take care of it?
Student: *Feed the puppy.*

Instructor: The third type of sentence is a question. **A question asks something.** It ends with a question mark. What question might your mother ask you when you came in from feeding the puppy?
Student: *Have you fed the puppy?* or *Did you feed the puppy?*

Instructor: The fourth type of sentence is an exclamation. **An exclamation shows sudden or strong feeling. It ends with an exclamation point.** What if you went out to feed the hungry, little puppy and discovered that it was a huge, hungry wolf? You might shout something to tell me that there was a wolf outside. What would you shout?
Student: *Help! There's a wolf outside!*

Instructor: That would certainly show strong feeling!

Verbs
Dictation exercise: "The Platypus"

Notes to Instructor: *You will need twenty-five index cards for the enrichment activity.*

Chant the preposition list twice today (this should take about ninety seconds): Aboard, about, above, across. After, against, along, among, around, at. Before, behind, below, beneath. Beside, between, beyond, by. Down, during, except, for, from. In, inside, into, like. Near, of, off, on, over. Past, since, through, throughout. To, toward, under, underneath. Until, up, upon. With, within, without.

Instructor: Let me repeat the definition of a verb for you. **A verb is a word that does an action, shows a state of being, links two words together, or helps another verb.** Can you say that definition back to me?

Note to Instructor: *If the student cannot repeat the definition back to you, say it with him three times.*

Instructor: I will give you some names of animals. Put an action verb with each one to tell me what sound each animal makes. Cows.
Student: *Cows moo.*

Instructor: Dogs…
Student: *Dogs bark.*

Instructor: Bears…
Student: *Bears growl.*

Instructor: Kittens…
Student: *Kittens meow.*

Instructor: A platypus…I bet you don't know what a platypus says. What is a platypus? A platypus is a small, furry mammal that lays eggs. It lives in the waters of Australia, and it has a bill like a duck. Why am I telling you this? I want you to listen to the sentence, "A platypus is a small, furry mammal." Does that sentence have an action verb in it?

Note to Instructor: *You may say each word of the sentence to the student and ask, "Can you do this? Can you "a"? Can you "platypus"? Can you "is"?" and so on.*

Instructor: What is the sentence about?
Student: *A platypus.*

Instructor: What does the sentence tell you about the platypus?
Student: *The platypus is a small, furry mammal.*

Instructor: The verb "is" links the word "platypus" to words that tell us more about the platypus. Remember, the linking verbs we have learned are the same as state of being verbs, but they are followed by information. It wouldn't be very interesting to say "The platypus is." You want to know more about it! Remember, state of being verbs become linking verbs if they link a word to other words which give more information about it. Repeat those verbs after me: Am, is, are, was, were. Be, being, been.

Note to Instructor: *If the student cannot say the list, repeat it with him five times.*

Instructor: There are four kinds of verbs: action verbs, state of being verbs, linking verbs, and helping verbs. Let's say the list of helping verbs together, beginning with "am, is, are, was, were."

Together: Am, is, are, was, were. Be, being, been. Have, has, had. Do, does, did. Shall, will, should, would, may, might, must. Can, could!

Note to Instructor: *If the student cannot repeat the list with you, say it with him twice more.*

Instructor: I know what a platypus says. A platypus can growl like a puppy and can cluck like a hen! Listen to me say that sentence one more time:

Note to Instructor: *Emphasize the words in bold print.*

Instructor: A platypus **can growl** like a puppy and **can cluck** like a hen. What kind of verb is "can"?
Student: *"Can" is a helping verb.*

Instructor: "Can" is helping the verb "growl." What kind of verb is "growl"? Is growling something you can do? Yes, you can growl. "Growl" is an action verb. What kind of verb is "cluck"?
Student: *"Cluck" is an action verb.*

Instructor: Now you have reviewed all four kinds of verbs and you have learned all sorts of interesting information! Did you know that a platypus is half the size of a cat and likes to eat frogs?

Dictation Exercise

Choose one of the following sentences.

The platypus is a furry mammal that lays eggs.

The platypus can growl like a puppy and can cluck like a hen.

Enrichment Activity

You will need twenty-five index cards. On the first five, write the linking verbs (one on each card): Am, is, are, was, were. On eight more cards, write the following eight words and phrases (one on each card):

The platypus

Forests

Red Riding Hood

Baby mice

Bulldozers

A pretzel

A clown

Beetles

On the last twelve cards, write the following words (one on each card):

furry

crunchy

squirmy

shady

creepy

adorable

powerful

stupid

silly

dangerous

orange

green

Help the student to combine the eight "subject cards" (nouns) with the twelve "descriptive cards" (adjectives) using the five linking verb cards to connect them. As you form each sentence, point out the linking verb to the student, and remind the student that the linking verb is connecting the two parts of the sentence together. Allow humorous combinations.

·················· **LESSON 79** ··················

Adverbs
Adjectives

Note to Instructor: *Chant the preposition list twice today (this should take about ninety seconds): Aboard, about, above, across. After, against, along, among, around, at. Before, behind, below, beneath. Beside, between, beyond, by. Down, during, except, for, from. In, inside, into, like. Near, of, off, on, over. Past, since, through, throughout. To, toward, under, underneath. Until, up, upon. With, within, without.*

Instructor: Do you remember the definition of an adjective? I will start you on it: An adjective is a word…

Student: *An adjective is a word that describes a noun or pronoun.*

Note to Instructor: *If the student cannot repeat this definition, say it with him three times.*

Instructor: Do you remember the definition of an adverb? I will start you on it: An adverb is a word…

Student: *An adverb is a word that describes a verb, an adjective, or another adverb.*

Note to Instructor: *If the student cannot repeat this definition, say it with him three times.*

Instructor: The names of animals are nouns, and adjectives describe nouns. I will give you the name of an animal, and I want you to think of some adjectives that describe it. Cow.

Note to Instructor: *You may suggest: black, white, red, friendly, large, small, tame, or wild.*

Instructor: In the last lesson, you told me that a cow moos. Now put your adjective together with the noun and verb to make a sentence.

Student: *The [adjective] cow moos.*

Instructor: Tell me an adverb that describes how the cow moos.

Note to Instructor: *You may suggest: loudly, softly, hungrily, forlornly, melodiously, lovingly, or lazily.*

Instructor: Now put that all together into one sentence.

Student: *The [adjective] cow moos [adverb].*

Instructor: The dog barks. Give me an adjective that describes the dog.

Note to Instructor: *You may suggest: furry, bouncy, sleek, hungry, strong, scruffy, flea-bitten, dirty, loving, or faithful.*

Instructor: Now put the adjective into your sentence.
Student: *The [adjective] dog barks.*

Instructor: Tell me an adverb that describes how the dog barks.

Note to Instructor: *You may suggest: loudly, suddenly, angrily, incessantly, ferociously, warningly, or bravely.*

Instructor: Now put that all together into one sentence.
Student: *The [adjective] dog barks [adverb].*

Instructor: A kitten meows. Give me an adjective that describes the kitten.

Note to Instructor: *You may suggest: tiny, fluffy, clean, soft, cuddly, sweet, gray, black, helpless, or playful.*

Instructor: Put the adjective into your sentence.
Student: *The [adjective] kitten meows.*

Instructor: Tell me an adverb that describes how the kitten meows.

Note to Instructor: *You may suggest: softly, weakly, innocently, frequently, timidly, or persistently.*

Instructor: Now put that all together into one sentence.
Student: *The [adjective] kitten meows [adverb].*

Instructor: Can you find the adjective in the following sentence? "The gentle wind blows through the trees."

Note to Instructor: *You may prompt the student by asking, "What kind of wind?"*

Student: *Gentle.*

Instructor: "Gentle" describes the noun "wind." "Wind" is a thing. Can you find the adjective in this sentence? Beautiful flowers bloom in the garden.

Note to Instructor: *You may prompt the student by asking, "What kind of flowers?"*

Student: *Beautiful.*

Instructor: "Beautiful" describes the noun "flowers." "Flowers" are things. Can you find the adverb in this sentence? The flowers sway gently in the breeze.

Note to Instructor: *You may prompt the student by asking, "The flowers sway how?"*

Student: Gently.

Instructor: "Gently" describes the action verb "sway." Now I will give you a sentence with both an adjective and an adverb in it. The adjective will describe a noun—a person, place, thing, or idea. The adverb will describe an action verb. I will say the sentence twice for you.

Instructor (twice): The weary runner sprinted bravely down the track.

Instructor: Can you find the adjective?

Note to Instructor: *You may prompt the student by asking, "Who is the sentence about? It is about a runner. Runner is a noun. What kind of runner?"*

Student: Weary.

Instructor: Can you find the adverb?

Note to Instructor: *You may prompt the student by asking, "What did the runner do? Sprinted. Sprinted is an action verb. The runner sprinted how?"*

Student: Bravely.

••••••••••••••••••• **LESSON 80** •••••••••••••••••••

Interjections
Prepositions
Dictation exercise: "Ow! Yuck! Oh!"
Poem review: "The Goops" (Lesson 2)

Notes to Instructor: *The student will need drawing supplies for the enrichment activity.*

Review "The Goops" today.

Instructor: I want you to read the following sentences from "The Three Bears" with me. I will read out loud as you follow along.

Goldilocks said to herself, "Oh! That is the most charming wood cottage with the most charming red roses and the most charming blue door."

"Ow!" she cried out. "That porridge is too hot!"

"Yuck!" she whined. "That porridge is too cold!"

"Mmm!" she exclaimed. "This porridge is neither too hot nor too cold. This is just right."

"Oh!" she complained, "That cushion is too hard!"

"Hmph!" she grumbled. "That cushion is too soft!"

"Ah!" she sighed. "This cushion is neither too hard nor too soft. This cushion is just right."

"Ooh!" she groaned. "That blanket is too thick!"

"Brrr," she shivered. "That blanket is too thin!"

"Mmm," she murmured. "This blanket is neither too thick nor too thin. This blanket is just right."

Instructor: Goldilocks talks to herself quite a lot! These short words express strong feeling. Do you remember what we call a word that expresses sudden or strong feeling?
Student: *An interjection.*

Instructor: Repeat that definition for me in a complete sentence: **An interjection is a word that expresses sudden or strong feeling.**
Student: *An interjection is a word that expresses sudden or strong feeling.*

Instructor: Let's read a few more sentences about Goldilocks from "The Three Bears."

She tasted the porridge in the big, blue bowl.

The chair had a big, blue cushion on the seat.

She threw the big, blue cushion under the chair.

Goldilocks liked the little bed with the yellow blanket.

Goldilocks saw a whole bear family beside her bed!

Instructor: Can you find the preposition in each sentence? Remember, **a preposition is a word that shows the relationship of a noun or pronoun to another word in the sentence.** Go through the preposition list in your mind and see whether you can find those words in these sentences. What is the preposition in the first sentence?

Student: *In.*

Note to Instructor: *If the student cannot find the preposition, ask "What word shows the relationship between the porridge and the big, blue bowl?"*

Instructor: "In" shows the relationship between the porridge and the big, blue, bowl. What is the preposition in the second sentence?

Note to Instructor: *If the student cannot find the preposition, ask "What word shows the relationship between the cushion and the seat?"*

Student: *On.*

Instructor: "On" shows the relationship between the cushion and the seat. What is the preposition in the third sentence?

Note to Instructor: *If the student cannot find the preposition, ask "What word shows the relationship between the cushion and the chair?"*

Student: *Under.*

Instructor: "Under" shows the relationship between the cushion and the chair. What is the preposition in the fourth sentence?

Note to Instructor: *If the student cannot find the preposition, ask "What word shows the relationship between the little bed and the yellow blanket?"*

Student: *With.*

Instructor: "With" shows the relationship between the little bed and the yellow blanket. What is the preposition in the fifth sentence?

Note to Instructor: *If the student cannot find the preposition, ask "What word shows the relationship between the bear family and the bed?"*

Student: *Beside.*

Instructor: "Beside" shows the relationship between the bear family and the bed.

Dictation Exercise

Choose one of these sentences that Goldilocks exclaims.

Ow! That porridge is too hot!

Yuck! That porridge is too cold!

Oh! That cushion is too hard!

Ah! This cushion is neither too hard nor too soft!

Oh! That is the most charming wood cottage with the most charming red roses and the most charming blue door!

Enrichment Activity

Have the student draw pictures of one or more of the following scenes and label each with the correct preposition.

the porridge in the big, blue bowl

the big, blue cushion on the seat of the chair

the big, blue cushion under the chair

the little bed with the yellow blanket

the whole bear family beside Goldilocks in the bed

LESSON 81

4/22/20

Direct and indirect quotations
Dictation exercise: "Who's that trip-trapping?"

Note to Instructor: *Chant the preposition list twice today (this should take about ninety seconds): Aboard, about, above, across. After, against, along, among, around, at. Before, behind, below, beneath. Beside, between, beyond, by. Down, during, except, for, from. In, inside, into, like. Near, of, off, on, over. Past, since, through, throughout. To, toward, under, underneath. Until, up, upon. With, within, without.*

Instructor: I am going to read you some quotes. See if you can tell me who says each one of these sentences.

Note to Instructor: *When reading these quotes, use a deep voice for Papa Bear and Great Big Billy Goat Gruff, a medium voice for Mama Bear and Middle-sized Billy Goat Gruff, and a little squeaky voice for Baby Bear and Little Billy Goat Gruff. The font size will remind you which is which. Do not show the student the quotes until you are finished. The purpose of the lesson is to fix in the student's mind that a direct quotation uses the <u>exact</u> words of the speaker.*

"Mmm. This blanket is neither too thick nor too thin. This blanket is just right." (Goldilocks)

"I'm coming to eat you up!" (the troll)

"Somebody has been eating my porridge!" (Papa Bear)

"Somebody has been eating my porridge!" (Mama Bear)

"Don't eat me. I'm just medium-sized. Wait for my brother. He is much fatter than I!" (Middle-sized Billy Goat Gruff)

"Somebody has been eating my porridge, and has eaten every last drop!" (Baby Bear)

"I'm so little that I'd hardly be a mouthful for you. Wait for my big brother. He is much fatter than I." (Little Billy Goat Gruff)

"Who's that trip-trapping over my bridge?" (the troll)

"Somebody has been sitting in my chair!" (Mama Bear)

"Someone has been sitting in my chair, and has broken the leg off!" (Baby Bear)

"Somebody has been sleeping in my bed!" (Papa Bear)

"Come on, then, and try to eat me!" (Great Big Billy Goat Gruff)

"Somebody has been sleeping in my bed, and she is still in it!" (Baby Bear)

Note to Instructor: *After you have read the quotes to the student and he has had a chance to identify them, show him the book. Point out the quotation marks on either side of the quotes.*

Instructor: Each one of these sentences is a direct quotation. These are the exact words spoken by the characters in the stories. A direct quotation has quotation marks on either side of it. An indirect quotation tells you what someone says but doesn't use their exact words. Look at the difference between these two sentences.

Note to Instructor: *Show the student the following two sentences.*

Little Billy Goat Gruff said, "Wait for my big brother. He is much fatter than I."

Little Billy Goat Gruff told the troll to wait for his big brother.

Instructor: Do you see the difference between the direct and indirect quotation? The direct quotation uses the actual words spoken by Little Billy Goat Gruff, but the indirect quotation just tells you the information that Little Billy Goat Gruff said. Look at the next two sentences. Can you tell me which is the direct quotation, and which is the indirect quotation?

Mama Bear complained that somebody had been eating her porridge.

Mama Bear said, "Somebody has been eating my porridge!"

Instructor: Can you tell me which of these sentences is a direct quotation? Which is an indirect quotation?

The troll said, "I'm coming to eat you up!"

The troll said that he would eat up Great Big Billy Goat Gruff.

Instructor: Remember, a direct quotation uses the exact words spoken by someone. It has quotation marks on either side of the actual words.

Dictation Exercise

Tell the student that each of the following sentences is a direct quotation and should have quotation marks on either side of it. If necessary, have the student practice making quotation marks before doing the dictation exercise. Choose one or more of the following quotes.

"I'm coming to eat you up!"

"Who's that trip-trapping over my bridge?"

"Someone has been sitting in my chair, and has broken the leg off!"

·   **LESSON 82**   ·

Nouns
Pronouns
Dictation exercise: "The Mother Cat"
Poem review: "The Little Bird" (Lesson 39)

4/23/20

Note to Instructor: *Review "The Little Bird" today.*

Instructor: Can you tell me the definition of a noun?
Student: *A noun is the name of a person, place, thing, or idea.*

Instructor: Listen carefully to this sentence. It has all four kinds of nouns in it: "The little girl, filled with excitement, peered into the kitchen to see her birthday cake on the counter." This sentence contains the name of a person, a place, a thing, and an idea. What kind of person is named in this sentence?
Student: *A little girl.*

Note to Instructor: *Repeat the sentence as needed.*

Instructor: What place is named in the sentence? The little girl peered into it.
Student: *The kitchen.*

Instructor: What thing is named in the sentence? The little girl wanted to see it!
Student: *The birthday cake.*

Instructor: What idea is named in the sentence? The little girl felt it as she peered into the kitchen.
Student: *Excitement.*

Instructor: Remember, an idea is something that you can think about in your mind, but can't see or touch. You can feel excitement in your mind but you can't see it or touch it. Now let's talk about another type of word. Listen to the sentence again. "The little girl, filled with excitement, peered into the kitchen to see her birthday cake on the counter." Do you remember what the word "her" is?

Note to Instructor: *If necessary, prompt the student for the answer.*

Student: *"Her" is a pronoun.*

Instructor: **A pronoun is a word used in the place of a noun.** Repeat that definition with me.

Together: **A pronoun is a word used in the place of a noun.**

198

Instructor:	I will read the pronouns to you while you listen.

I, me, my, mine.
You, your, yours.
He, she, him, her, it, his, hers, its.
We, us, our, ours.
They, them, their, theirs.

Instructor:	Listen to me while I say the sentence again. "The little girl, filled with excitement, peered into the kitchen to see her birthday cake on the counter." This time, I will put a pronoun in place of one of the nouns. "The little girl peered into the kitchen, full of excitement, to see it on the counter." Which noun did I replace with a pronoun?
Student:	*The birthday cake* [or *cake*].

Instructor:	"It" is a pronoun that stands for the noun "cake." Listen one more time: "Filled with excitement, she peered into the kitchen to see her birthday cake on the counter." Which noun did I replace with a pronoun?
Student:	*The little girl* [or *girl*].

Instructor:	"She" is a pronoun that stands for the noun "girl." I am going to read you several sentences, and I want you to repeat them back to me. Here is the sentence: "Sam forgot to water the flowers." Repeat it back to me.
Student:	*Sam forgot to water the flowers.*

Instructor:	Sam forgot to water them.
Student:	*Sam forgot to water them.*

Instructor:	The girls will wrap a present for their brother.
Student:	*The girls will wrap a present for their brother.*

Instructor:	They will wrap a present for him.
Student:	*They will wrap a present for him.*

Instructor:	What noun did we replace with the pronoun "him"?
Student:	*Their brother* [or *brother*].

Instructor:	The woman cooked a huge meal.
Student:	*The woman cooked a huge meal.*

Instructor:	She cooked it.
Student:	*She cooked it.*

Instructor:	Who is "she"?

Student: *The woman* [or *woman*].

Instructor: What is "it"?
Student: *The meal* [or *meal*].

Instructor: The man gave money to the poor people.
Student: *The man gave money to the poor people.*

Instructor: He gave it to them.
Student: *He gave it to them.*

Instructor: Who is "he"?
Student: *The man* [or *man*].

Instructor: What is "it"?
Student: *The money* [or *money*].

Instructor: Who is "them"?
Student: *The poor people* [or *people*].

Dictation Exercise

Choose one of the following pairs of sentences.

The mother cat licked the kittens. She licked them.

The children played with the puppy. They played with it.

Paul Revere rode his horse to warn the people. He rode it to warn them.

4/24/20

•••••••••••••••••••••   **LESSON 83**   ••••••••••••••••••••

Contractions
Copywork: Contractions

Note to Instructor: *Chant the preposition list twice today (this should take about ninety seconds): Aboard, about, above, across. After, against, along, among, around, at. Before, behind, below, beneath. Beside, between, beyond, by. Down, during, except, for, from. In, inside, into, like. Near, of, off, on, over. Past, since, through, throughout. To, toward, under, underneath. Until, up, upon. With, within, without.*

Instructor: I will tell you a story today, and you will say one line of it over and over again with me. Once upon a time, an old woman made a man out of gingerbread. She put him in the oven, but when he started to bake he jumped up and ran away. Do you know what he said when he ran? Say it with me.

Together: Run, run, as fast as you can. You can't catch me. I'm the gingerbread man.

Instructor: You are using contractions when you say the gingerbread man's line. "Can't" and "I'm" are contractions. They are short forms of the words "cannot" and "I am." A contraction is made up of two words, put together into one word, with some letters left out. A punctuation mark called an apostrophe is put in the place of the missing letters. Now say: "Run, run, as fast as you can. You <u>cannot</u> catch me. <u>I am</u> the gingerbread man."

Student: *Run, run, as fast as you can. You cannot catch me. I am the gingerbread man.*

Instructor: The gingerbread man passed a cow, and the cow said, "You'll be a lovely meal! Stop and let me eat you!" The cow was using a contraction, too. "You'll" is short for "You will." Say, "<u>You will</u> be a lovely meal."

Student: *You will be a lovely meal.*

Instructor: And the gingerbread man said—say it with me—

Together: Run, run, as fast as you can. You can't catch me. I'm the gingerbread man.

Instructor: The gingerbread man passed two farmers, and the farmers said, "Wouldn't it be nice to eat that gingerbread man?" They could have said, "<u>Would not</u> it be nice to eat that gingerbread man?" But they were in a hurry. They called out, "Stop so we can eat you!" And the gingerbread man said:

Together: Run, run, as fast as you can. You can't catch me. I'm the gingerbread man.

Instructor: Then the gingerbread man came to a stream. He couldn't cross it, but a fox came along and said, "I'll carry you across." "I'll" is a contraction of what two words?

Student: *I will.*

Note to Instructor: *Prompt student for the answer, if necessary.*

Instructor: So the gingerbread man jumped on the fox's back. But when the fox plunged into the water, the gingerbread man started to get wet. He climbed up on the fox's nose and… what happened then?

Student: *The fox ate him.*

Instructor: And then the fox licked his lips and said, "I'm so glad I had that lovely snack." "I'm" is a contraction of what two words?

Student: *I am.*

Note to Instructor: *Prompt student for the answer, if necessary. In the following exercise, if the student is unable to think of the correct contraction, say it for him and ask him to repeat it after you.*

Instructor: I will say two or three words for you, and I want you to make each set of words into a contraction.

Instructor: He is
Student: *He's*

Instructor: She is
Student: *She's*

Instructor: It is
Student: *It's*

Instructor: We will
Student: *We'll*

Instructor: You are
Student: *You're*

Instructor: I cannot
Student: *I can't*

Instructor: She will not
Student: *She won't*

Instructor: He does not
Student: *He doesn't*

Instructor: They were not
Student: *They weren't*

Copywork

Ask the student to copy the following list onto his own paper in two straight columns.

are not   aren't

were not   weren't

should not   shouldn't

could not   couldn't

would not   wouldn't

············   **LESSON 84**   ······················

Picture Narration: "Snap the Whip," by Winslow Homer

Instructor: Look at the picture while I tell you about the artist, Winslow Homer. He was an American painter who died in 1910, about a hundred years ago. He painted scenes of the country and the sea. In this painting, boys are playing during recess from school. This game is called "Snap the Whip." All of the players hold hands in a long line, and the player at the head of the line runs quickly back and forth, changing direction as fast as possible. The players at the end of the line get thrown back and forth, like the end of a whip when you crack it in the air.

In the picture, how many boys are playing this game?

Student: *There are eight boys playing the game.*

Instructor: What do you think has happened to the two boys at the end of the line?

Student: *They fell down when the whip snapped.*

Instructor: Do you think that the boys were running fast or slow?

Student: *They were running very fast.*

Instructor: What is the building behind the boys?

Student: *The building is the school.*

Instructor: Which boy do you think is the leader?

Student: *[Points to the boy on the right-hand side of the picture.]*

Instructor: What time of year do you think it is?

Student: *It is spring.*

Instructor: How do you know?

Student: *The boys are barefoot [or any other reasonable explanation].*

Instructor: Describe what one of the boys is wearing. Those were school clothes, a hundred years ago!

Student: *The boy is wearing a jacket, a hat, suspenders, and pants [any combination].*

Note to Instructor: *You can view this painting in full color online at http://www.winslow-homer.com/Snap-the-Whip-I.html.*

······················ **LESSON 85** ······················

Poem memorization: "All Things Bright and Beautiful"

Note to Instructor: *Read the entire poem aloud to the student. Then read only the first two stanzas three times. Repeat this process later in the day.*

All Things Bright and Beautiful
By Cecil Alexander

All things bright and beautiful,
All creatures great and small,
All things wise and wonderful,
The Lord God made them all.

Each little flower that opens,
Each little bird that sings,
He made their glowing colors,
He made their tiny wings.

The purple-headed mountain,
The river running by,
The sunset, and the morning,
That brighten up the sky;

The cold wind in the winter,
The pleasant summer sun,
The ripe fruits in the garden,
He made them every one.

The tall trees in the greenwood,
The meadows where we play,
The rushes by the water,
We gather every day;

He gave us eyes to see them,
And lips that we might tell
How great is God Almighty,
Who has made all things well.

5/1/20

• • • • • • • • • • • • • • • • • • •   **LESSON 86**   • • • • • • • • • • • • • • • • • •

Cumulative review

Instructor: In the last lesson, we read a very long and serious poem. For this lesson, we are going to read a very short and silly poem. I will read it as you follow along.

The Old Man and His Nose
By Edward Lear

There was an old man with a nose,

Who said, "If you choose to suppose,

That my nose is too long,

You are certainly wrong!"

That remarkable man with a nose.

Instructor: This poem uses many of the capitalization and punctuation rules you have learned. What is the title of this poem?

Student: *"The Old Man and His Nose."*

Instructor: You have learned that you should capitalize the first word and every important word in the titles of poems, stories, or books. What is the only unimportant word in this title?

Student: *And.*

Instructor: "And" is a conjunction. I will start you on the definition of a conjunction and you will finish it. **A conjunction joins**…

Student: *A conjunction joins words or groups of words together.*

Instructor: Conjunctions are usually considered "unimportant" words when they are in titles. Who wrote this poem?

Student: *Edward Lear*

Instructor: "Edward" and "Lear" are both proper names. Repeat after me: Proper names begin with capital letters.

Student: *Proper names begin with capital letters.*

Instructor: Look at the poem at the beginning of the lesson. Then look at the same poem written below. What is different?

there was an old man with a nose,

who said, "If you choose to suppose,

that my nose is too long,

you are certainly wrong!"

that remarkable man with a nose.

Note to Instructor: *If the student cannot see the differences, point to the first letter in each line.*

Student: *The beginning letters of the lines are not capitalized.*

Instructor: Repeat after me: Capitalize the beginning of every line in poetry.
Student: *Capitalize the beginning of every line in poetry.*

Instructor: Look back at the poem at the beginning of the lesson (the properly capitalized poem!). Find the exact words that the old man says. They will have quotation marks around them. Read me those lines in a funny old-man voice!
Student: *"If you choose to suppose, that my nose is too long, you are certainly wrong!"*

Instructor: The exact words a person says are always enclosed by quotation marks. I think that this old man feels strongly about his nose. What mark of punctuation in the poem shows you that he feels strongly?
Student: *The exclamation point.*

Instructor: An exclamation shows sudden or strong feeling. It ends with an exclamation point! Look at the first line of the poem again. The word "man" is a noun. What is a noun?
Student: *A noun is the name of a person, place, thing, or idea.*

Instructor: Is "man" a person, place, thing, or idea?
Student: *A person.*

Instructor: "Old" tells us what *kind* of man he is. It describes the noun "man." What do we call a word that describes a noun?
Student: *An adjective is a word that describes a noun.*

Instructor: "Old" comes right before "man" in the first line. In the third line of the poem, there is another adjective. It describes "nose," but instead of coming just before "nose," it comes after the verb. Can you find the adjective I'm talking about?

Student: Long.

Instructor: Sometimes adjectives come later in the sentence, after a linking verb. Can you find the linking verb in the third line?

Student: Is.

Instructor: Tell me the definition of a verb. I will get you started. **A verb is a word that...**

Student: *A verb is a word that does an action, shows a state of being, links two words together, or helps another verb.*

Enrichment Activity

The student may draw a picture of the man and his long nose!

5/4/20

· · · · · · · · · · · · · · · · · · ·   **LESSON 87**   · · · · · · · · · · · · · · · · · ·

Cumulative review

Instructor: Are you ready for your grammar lesson today?
Student: *Yes.*

Instructor: That didn't sound very excited. Let me hear you say "Yes!" as if you were really excited about doing this lesson! Shout it out with sudden and strong emotion!
Student: *Yes!*

Instructor: That sounded like it had an exclamation point after it! Write an exclamation point on your paper!

Instructor: I started out this lesson by asking you a question. Do you remember what kind of punctuation mark comes at the end of a question?
Student: *A question mark.*

Instructor: Write a question mark on your paper.

Note to Instructor: *Help the student write a beautiful question mark. Then clasp your hands together and say "Wow!" very loudly. Try to startle the student!*

Instructor: I said "Wow!" because your question mark was so beautiful. It made me have sudden and strong feelings. "Wow" is an interjection. **An interjection is a word that expresses sudden or strong feeling.** Say that definition for me.
Student: *An interjection is a word that expresses sudden or strong feeling.*

Instructor: I want you to write the word "Wow!" on your paper. Remember this rule: An interjection all alone with an exclamation point should begin with a capital letter.

Note to Instructor: *Watch the student write "Wow!" on his paper. If he forgets to capitalize the word, remind him!*

Instructor: I will tell you something interesting about the word "wow." In the country of Scotland, "wow" is an action verb. Look at the definition of the verb "wow" and follow along as I read.

wow: to howl, wail, bark, whine, or meow

Instructor: How many verbs are in the definition?
Student: *There are five verbs.*

Instructor: They are written in a series. Point to the commas that come between each item in the series. Now repeat after me: Put commas between items in a series.
Student: *Put commas between items in a series.*

Instructor: Can you howl loudly for me?
Student: *[howls]*

Instructor: Can you meow softly for me?
Student: *[meows]*

Instructor: Can you whine sadly for me?
Student: *[whines]*

Instructor: Can you bark repeatedly for me?
Student: *[barks]*

Instructor: "Loudly," "softly," "sadly," and "repeatedly" are all adverbs that describe the verbs "howl," "meow," "whine," and "bark." I will start you on the definition of an adverb, and you will finish it for me. **An adverb is a word that describes**...
Student: *An adverb is a word that describes a verb, an adjective, or another adverb.*

LESSON 88

Cumulative review

Instructor: In the last two lessons, we reviewed many of the definitions and rules you learned this year. Today we will review the rest of them. Let's begin with the definition of a pronoun. We have said over and over again that a noun is the name of a person, place, thing, or idea. Do you remember what a pronoun is?

Note to Instructor: *Prompt the student if necessary.*

Student: *A pronoun is a word used in place of a noun.*

Instructor: I will read you four sentences. Follow along with me as I read.

On March 7, 2010, Mr. J. Smith and I went out to fly a kite.

The day was warm, because it was spring.

The weather was so windy that I couldn't hold on to the kite!

The kite blew away and ended up in Philadelphia, Pennsylvania.

Instructor: The first sentence is a statement. What kind of punctuation mark ends the statement?
Student: *A period.*

Instructor: A statement ends with a period. There are also two periods in the middle of the sentence. The first one comes after an abbreviated title of respect. What is the title of respect?
Student: *Mr.*

Instructor: Abbreviated titles of respect are capitalized and followed by periods. The second period in the middle of the sentence comes after the initial "J." Repeat after me: Initials are capitalized and followed by periods.
Student: *Initials are capitalized and followed by periods.*

Instructor: Point to the date in the first sentence. The names of months should always be capitalized. What month is capitalized in the first sentence?
Student: *March.*

Instructor: *On what day in March did this story take place?*
Student: *March 7.*

Instructor: In what year?
Student: *2010.*

Instructor: Point to the comma between the 7 and the 2010. Repeat after me: In a date, a comma separates the day of the month and the year.
Student: *In a date, a comma separates the day of the month and the year.*

Instructor: During what season did this story take place?
Student: *Spring.*

Instructor: Is spring capitalized?
Student: *No.*

Instructor: We capitalize the names of the months, but not the names of the seasons. In the third sentence, who couldn't hold on to the kite?
Student: *I couldn't hold on to the kite.*

Instructor: Point to the pronoun "I" and repeat after me: The pronoun "I" is always capitalized.
Student: *The pronoun "I" is always capitalized.*

Instructor: Point to the word "couldn't." This word is a contraction. Repeat after me: A contraction is two words put together into one word with some letters left out.
Student: *A contraction is two words put together into one word with some letters left out.*

Instructor: Look at the two words below. Point to the letter that has been left out of the contraction.

could not   couldn't

Instructor: The letter "o" was left out. What punctuation mark is put in the place of the missing "o"?
Student: *An apostrophe.*

Instructor: Where did the kite end up?
Student: *Philadelphia, Pennsylvania.*

Instructor: Repeat this final rule after me: In an address, a comma separates the name of a city from the name of a state.
Student: *In an address, a comma separates the name of a city from the name of a state.*

•••••••••••••••••••••   **LESSON 89**   •••••••••••••••••••••

Prepositions
Poem review: "All Things Bright and Beautiful" (Lesson 85)

5/6/20

Note to Instructor: *Read "All Things Bright and Beautiful" once through. Read the first four stanzas one more time. Then read the fifth and sixth stanzas three times in a row.*

Instructor: Repeat after me: **A preposition is a word that shows the relationship of a noun or pronoun to another word in the sentence.**

Student: *A preposition is a word that shows the relationship of a noun or pronoun to another word in the sentence.*

Instructor: I will say our list of prepositions, and then we will say them together two more times. "Aboard, about, above, across. After, against, along, among, around, at. Before, behind, below, beneath. Beside, between, beyond, by. Down, during, except, for, from. In, inside, into, like. Near, of, off, on, over. Past, since, through, throughout. To, toward, under, underneath. Until, up, upon. With, within, without."

Together (twice): Aboard, about, above, across. After, against, along, among, around, at. Before, behind, below, beneath. Beside, between, beyond, by. Down, during, except, for, from. In, inside, into, like. Near, of, off, on, over. Past, since, through, throughout. To, toward, under, underneath. Until, up, upon. With, within, without.

Instructor: I will read you some sentences. Wherever there is a preposition, I will say the word "preposition." I want you to repeat the sentence back to me, and put a real preposition in that blank. For example, if I say "Mandy is preposition her desk," you will say back to me "Mandy is at her desk."

Note to Instructor: *The student's answers are suggested, but any appropriate preposition from the list is acceptable. If the student is unable to answer, begin to repeat the list back to him, one preposition at a time, asking him to try each preposition. (Generally this will spark his imagination so that you will not have to continue on through the whole list.)*

Instructor: There is a ceiling [preposition] Mandy's head.
Student: *There is a ceiling <u>above</u> Mandy's head.*

Instructor: The dog chased the cat [preposition] the house.
Student: *The dog chased the cat <u>into</u> [or out of] the house.*

Instructor: The baby threw its pacifier [preposition] the sofa.
Student: *The baby threw its pacifier <u>under</u> [or behind] the sofa.*

Instructor: When Linus vacuumed, he found balls of dust [preposition] his bed.

Student: *When Linus vacuumed, he found balls of dust <u>under</u> his bed.*

Instructor: We will do school [preposition] lunchtime.

Student: *We will do school <u>until</u> [or after] lunchtime.*

Instructor: Take your hat [preposition] when you come inside.

Student: *Take your hat <u>off</u> when you come inside.*

Instructor: The train sped [preposition] the tunnel.

Student: *The train sped <u>through</u> the tunnel.*

Instructor: I like pancakes [preposition] maple syrup.

Student: *I like pancakes <u>with</u> maple syrup.*

Instructor: Do not cram your mouth [preposition] too much food!

Student: *Do not cram your mouth <u>with</u> too much food!*

• • • • • • • • • • • • • • • • • • • **LESSON 90** • • • • • • • • • • • • • • • • •

Synonyms

Antonyms

5/7/20

Dictation exercise: "The troll"

Poem review: "All Things Bright and Beautiful" (Lesson 85)

Note to Instructor: *Read "All Things Bright and Beautiful" three times through.*

Instructor: Do you remember that "ssssynonyms have the sssssame meaning"? Listen to me repeat the definition of a synonym, and then we will say it together: **Synonyms are words that have the same meaning.**

Together: **Synonyms are words that have the same meaning.**

Instructor: **Antonyms are opposites.** Let's say that together three times: **Antonyms are opposites.**

Together (three times): **Antonyms are opposites.**

Instructor: Now, we will read several lists of synonyms together. For each list, I will give you a sentence. I want you to say the sentence back to me three times, each time choosing a different synonym for the word I emphasize.

Note to Instructor: *In the following exercises, allow the student to look at the list of synonyms given as he repeats the sentence three times, substituting different synonyms for the italicized word you emphasize.*

Instructor: I will do the first one for you. Let's read the list of synonyms:

Together: Pretty, beautiful, lovely, gorgeous.

Instructor: Here is the sentence. "The sunset was *pretty.*" You would say back to me "The sunset was *beautiful.* The sunset was *lovely.* The sunset was *gorgeous.*" Read those sentences.

Student reads: The sunset was beautiful. The sunset was lovely. The sunset was gorgeous.

Instructor: Now, let's read a second list of synonyms together:

Together: Ugly, frightful, horrible, unsightly, dreadful, hideous.

Instructor: Here is the sentence for you to practice substituting different synonyms for a word: "The troll who lived under the bridge was certainly ugly." I want you to say the sentence back to me three times, each time choosing a different synonym for the word "ugly."

Student: *The troll was [synonym]. The troll was [synonym]. The troll was [synonym].*

Instructor: If you were a troll, you might not see the troll as ugly. You might see him as handsome.

Here are some antonyms for "ugly." They are the opposite of "ugly." Remember, antonyms are opposites. Read these antonyms for "ugly" with me.

TOGETHER: Beautiful, handsome, lovely, pretty, comely, good-looking, attractive.

Instructor: Here is a sentence that you will say back to me three times: "The troll who lived under the bridge was certainly good-looking." Each time, choose a different word from the list we just read.

Student: *The troll was certainly [synonym]. The troll was certainly [synonym]. The troll was certainly [synonym].*

Instructor: Let's read another list of synonyms:

TOGETHER: Bite, chew, gnash, chomp, nibble, munch.

Instructor: Here is the sentence to say back to me three times, using a different synonym: "The troll wanted to bite the Great Big Billy Goat Gruff."

Student: *The troll wanted to [synonym] the Great Big Billy Goat Gruff. The troll wanted to [synonym] the Great Big Billy Goat Gruff. The troll wanted to [synonym] the Great Big Billy Goat Gruff.*

Instructor: Let's practice a few more antonyms. For each sentence that I say to you, tell me the opposite. I am sad.

Student: *I am happy.*

Instructor: I am awake.
Student: *I am asleep.*

Instructor: This room is quiet.
Student: *This room is noisy.*

Instructor: The sun is up.
Student: *The sun is down.*

Instructor: The sky is light.
Student: *The sky is dark.*

Instructor: You have done an excellent job of contradicting me!

Dictation Exercise

Dictate one of the following pairs of sentences to the student. Tell the student that you will stop at a period for the count of five, and that you will draw your breath before beginning the next sentence.

The troll liked goats. He relished them.

The goats would taste delicious. They would taste yummy.

The goats tricked the foolish troll. They outwitted him and got away.

Enrichment Activity

Ask the student to make up sentences using the following synonym sets:

Set 1
warble, sing, carol, whistle, trill, twitter, tweet (think birds!)

Set 2
wiggly, squirmy, jumpy, jerky, twitchy, fidgety

Set 3
fancy, colored, decorated, befrilled, flowery, ornate, embellished

•••••••••••••••••••••••••   **LESSON 91**   ••••••••••••••••••••

5/8/20

Parts of speech review
Poem review: "All Things Bright and Beautiful" (Lesson 85)

Notes to Instructor: *Read "All Things Bright and Beautiful" out loud once. Ask the student to recite the poem from memory. Stop and read out loud three times any stanza that he finds difficult.*

Read the following paragraph aloud together.

TOGETHER:

Robin Hood crept carefully through the forest. He was looking for a rich traveller with much gold. Robin Hood could take his gold, and give it to an old, poor woman. The old woman would thank him and weep with joy. "Oh!" she would say. "I am a happy woman!"

Note to Instructor: *Tell the student that every word in the above paragraph is one of the following:*

noun

pronoun

adjective

verb (action, linking, helping)

adverb

preposition

article

conjunction

interjection

Note to Instructor: *Allow the student to look at this list as he identifies each word in the paragraph. A key for the instructor follows.*

Key for the Instructor

Robin Hood	noun (proper name)
crept	verb
carefully	adverb
through	preposition
the	article
forest	noun
He	pronoun

was	helping verb
looking	action verb
for	preposition
a	article
rich	adjective
traveller	noun
with	preposition
much	adjective
gold	noun
Robin Hood	noun (proper name)
could	helping verb
take	action verb
his	pronoun
gold	noun
and	conjunction
give	action verb
it	pronoun
to	preposition
an	article
old	adjective
poor	adjective
woman	noun
The	article
old	adjective
woman	noun
would	helping verb
thank	action verb
him	pronoun
and	conjunction
weep	action verb
with	preposition
joy	noun (idea)
Oh	interjection
she	pronoun
would	helping verb
say	action verb
I	pronoun
am	linking verb
a	article
happy	adjective
woman	noun

• **LESSON 92** •

Picture narration: "One of the Family" by Frederick George Cotman

Instructor: Look at the picture while I tell you about the artist, Frederick George Cotman. He was born in England in 1850, over a hundred and fifty years ago, and lived there his whole life. He liked to paint everyday scenes of life in England. In this painting, a family meal has an unexpected guest! Who is the guest?

Student: *The guest is a horse!*

Instructor: The horse isn't the only animal at the meal, is he? What other animal is "one of the family"?

Student: *The dog is one of the family too.*

Instructor: Now, let's see some of your prepositions. List four things that are **on** the table.

Student: *Plates, a jug, glasses, a pie, silverware, food, and napkins are on the table.*

Instructor: Tell me who is **around** the table.

Student: *The mother, the grandmother, and the children are around the table.*

Instructor: What are they sitting **on**?

Student: *They are sitting on chairs.*

Instructor: Who is **in** the corner?

Student: *The father is in the corner.*

Instructor: Where is the horse—**outside** the door or **inside** the door?

Student: *The horse is outside the door.*

Instructor: Where is the horse's head?

Student: *The horse's head is inside the door.*

Instructor: How did the horse get his head inside?

Student: *He poked it through [over] the door.*

Instructor: Do you think the horse would like to come all the way **into** the house?

Student: *I think he would.*

Note to Instructor: *You can view this painting in full color at a number of online art sites, including all-posters.com (http://www.allposters.com/-st/Frederick-George-Cotman-Posters_c78640_.htm) or art.com (http://www.art.com/products/p10290576-sa-i852862/one_of_the_family.htm).*

···············   **LESSON 93**   ······················

Review of memorized lists

Instructor: You have already reviewed the list of all the prepositions. Today we are going to review the other lists we have memorized. I want you to get up and shake your arms and warm up your legs, because you're going to have to move around!

Instructor: Let's begin with the state of being verbs. Remember, these can also be used as linking verbs. Listen as I say them for you: "am, is, are, was, were, be, being, been." Now I want you to say that list. But I want you to pretend that you are a robot. For every state of being verb, move your arms and head as though you were a robot!

Student: *Am, is, are, was, were, be, being, been.*

Instructor: Now I want you to say the whole list of helping verbs. Turn so that you are facing away from me and march as you say the list. Take one step for each helping verb. When you are finished, shout back and tell me where you are!

Student: *[marching] Am, is, are, was, were, be, being, been. Have, has, had, do, does, did, shall, will, should, would, may, might, must, can, could.*

Note to Instructor: *You may have to follow the student if he needs prompting!*

Instructor: Now recite the list of articles: a, an, the. As you say each article, jump up and turn in a circle!

Student: *[jumps up and turns in circles] A, an, the.*

Instructor: Your last list is the list of conjunctions. This only has three words on it: and, but, or. Crouch down, and as you say each conjunction, take a huge frog leap forward. How far can you get?

Student: *[leaping] And, but, or.*

•   **LESSON 94**   • • • • • • • • • • • • • • • • • • •

Homophones
Poem review: "All Things Bright and Beautiful" (Lesson 85)

Notes to Instructor: *Read "All Things Bright and Beautiful" out loud once. Ask the student to recite the poem from memory. Stop and read out loud three times any stanza that he finds difficult.*

There is some disagreement about the terms "homophone" and "homonym." In this lesson, we will follow the majority of experts and use "homophone" to mean any two words that sound alike but have different meanings. Homophones may be spelled differently, as in bear *and* bare, *or spelled alike, as in* light *(not dark) and* light *(not heavy). Homophones which are spelled alike are often known by the more specific name "homonyms." Homonyms are covered in Level 3 of* First Language Lessons. *Second graders do not yet need to learn these definitions, but it is helpful for them to know that there can be more than one way to spell words that sound the same.*

Instructor: We have already learned about synonyms and antonyms. **Synonyms are words that have the same meaning**, while **antonyms are words that have opposite meanings**. Today we're going to learn about a third kind of word: **homophones**! As I read you this poem, follow along.

The Tutor
By Carolyn Wells

A **tutor** who tooted the flute

Tried to teach two young **tooters** to toot.

Said the two to the **tutor,**

"Is it harder to toot, or

To **tutor** two **tooters** to toot?"

Instructor: Now read all of the words in bold letters out loud.
Student: *Tutor, tooters, tutor, tutor, tooters!*

Instructor: The words "tutor" and "tooter" sound the same. But they are spelled differently, and they have different meanings. A "tutor" is a teacher. A "tooter" is someone who toots a flute! When words sound the same—even though they have different meanings—they are called homophones. Now look at this second version of the poem:

A tutor who tooted the flute

Tried **to** teach **two** young tooters **to** toot.

Said the **two to** the tutor,

"Is it harder **to** toot, or

To tutor **two** tooters **to** toot?"

Instructor: Read all of the words in bold letters out loud.
Student: *To, two, to, two, to, to, To, two, to!*

Instructor: "Two" means "more than one and less than three." "To" doesn't! Let's look at a few other homophones. First, read me the two homophones. Then follow along as I read you a sentence that reminds you what each word means.

STUDENT		INSTRUCTOR
bare	bear	Without his fur, a bear would be bare!
pail	pale	Jack looked pale when Jill dropped her pail.
eight	ate	I ate eight doughnuts.
read	red	Yesterday I read a red book.
be	bee	The bee might be angry!
hay	hey	Hey, don't forget to give the horse his hay.
hear	here	Don't shout; I can hear you because I'm right here!
right	write	Is there a right way to write the letter A?
whole	hole	I dropped my whole cookie down that hole!
sea	see	When we go to the beach, I see the sea.
blew	blue	I blew up a blue balloon and it blew away.
knight	night	One night, a brave knight rode out to fight a dragon.
knot	not	Do not tie a knot, or you will not be able to unknot it!
tail	tale	Tell me the tale of why the bear has a short tail.

5/13/20

••••••••••••••••••••••• **LESSON 95** •••••••••••••••••

Cumulative poem review

Instructor: Today we are going to review all of the poems you have memorized so far. When we recite a poem, we begin with the title and author. I will give you the title and author for each poem. Say the title and author back to me, and then recite the poem. Remember, stand up straight! Don't fidget while you're reciting! And speak in a nice, loud, slow voice.

Note to Instructor: *You may prompt as necessary. If the student repeats the poem accurately, move on to the next poem. If he stumbles, ask him to repeat the line he cannot remember three times.*

Lesson	Poem	Author
2	"The Goops"	Gelett Burgess
31	"The Year"	Sara Coleridge, adapted by Sara Buffington
39	"The Little Bird"	Mother Goose rhyme
51	"The Months"	Mother Goose rhyme
85	"All Things Bright and Beautiful"	Cecil Alexander

Note to Instructor: *You may also read back through the poems which were not memorized.*

"The Wind"	Lesson 15
"Against Quarrelling and Fighting"	Lesson 26
"How Creatures Move"	Lesson 29
"Whole Duty of Children"	Lesson 48
"Days of the Week"	Lesson 51
"Bed in Summer" (one stanza)	Lesson 61
"The Daffodils" (one stanza)	Lesson 63
"I Love You Well"	Lesson 66
"Foreign Lands"	Lesson 72
"The Old Man and His Nose"	Lesson 86
"The Tutor"	Lesson 94

5/15/20 • • • • • • • • • • • • • • • • • • **LESSON 96** • • • • • • • • • • • • • • • •

Dictation exercise: Review session 1

Instructor: For each of the next three lessons, I will dictate three sentences to you. These sentences will include many of the rules we have studied. Remember, I will pause briefly whenever I reach a comma. I will pause and count to five whenever I reach a period, and I will take a breath before beginning the next sentence.

Note to Instructor: *If you see the student writing some part of the sentence incorrectly, stop him and remind him of the appropriate rule. He should do these sentences in pencil so that he can erase and make immediate corrections. Don't frustrate the student. Adjust your speed of dictation to the student's ability.*

My brother and I play soccer.

We play on Tuesdays, Thursdays, and Saturdays in the summer.

In the fall, we play other teams.

········· **LESSON 97** ····················

Dictation exercise: Review session 2   5/15/20

Instructor: The dictation sentences in today's lesson will include many of the rules we have studied. Remember, I will pause briefly whenever I reach a comma. I will pause and count to five whenever I reach a period, and I will take a breath before beginning the next sentence. If one of the sentences is an exclamation, I will sound excited as I dictate it.

Note to Instructor: *If you see the student writing some part of the sentence incorrectly, stop him and remind him of the appropriate rule. He should do these sentences in pencil so that he can erase and make immediate corrections. Make sure to read the exclamation with an excited voice. For long words, help the student sound the words out syllable by syllable. Give all necessary help with spelling. Don't frustrate the student. Adjust your speed of dictation to the student's ability.*

On July 4, 1776, the states declared independence.

Mr. Ellis sets off fireworks on the Fourth of July.

They fizzle and spark!

Dictation exercise: Review session 3

5/18/20

Instructor: The dictation sentences in today's lesson will include many of the rules we have studied. I will pause and count to five whenever I reach a period, and I will take a breath before beginning the next sentence.

Note to Instructor: *If you see the student writing some part of the sentence incorrectly, stop him and remind him of the appropriate rule. He should do these sentences in pencil so that he can erase and make immediate corrections. Give all necessary help in spelling. Don't frustrate the student. Adjust your speed of dictation to the student's ability.*

Would you like a cookie?

Mrs. R. L. Brown made cookies for us.

Aren't they wonderful?

· · · · · · · · · · · · · · · · · · ·   **LESSON 99**   · · · · · · · · · · · · · · · ·

Story narration: "The Donkey and the Salt"

5/19/20

Note to Instructor: *Read the following story aloud to the student. Then ask the "starter questions" at the end of the story. Remember to encourage the student to answer in complete sentences. Then ask the student, "What is one thing you remember from the story?" Write his answer down and read it back to him.*

The Donkey and the Salt
A Folktale

A merchant who lived long ago often heaped huge bags of salt upon his donkey's back and drove the donkey to the market. There, he would sell the salt for a good price. He was happy—but his donkey was discontent. The salt was tremendously heavy. And although the money that the merchant earned at the market bought the donkey good grain and sweet hay, the donkey complained about his work. "If only I didn't have to haul these bags of salt!" he moaned. "My life would be so much easier!"

On his way to the market one day, the donkey stumbled on a little bridge over a stream and fell into the water. As he lay in the water, the salt melted and ran away down the stream. "Get up," the merchant ordered. When the donkey scrambled to his feet, the bags were empty. He felt light and carefree! He switched his tail and trotted happily down the road, free of his burden.

The merchant was sad, for he made no money at the market. He returned home with empty hands. "What will I do?" he asked himself. "Without my market days, I will no longer be able to buy grain and hay for my donkey."

But the donkey was pleased with his day off. On his next trip to the market, he stumbled again—this time on purpose! He rolled into the water and waited for the salt to melt. When the bags were empty once more, he jumped to his feet and ambled cheerfully along. "Hurrah!" he thought to himself. "I am free of my burden *again*! Now I know the secret. I don't ever have to carry salt to the market again."

The merchant realized that his lazy donkey had fallen on purpose. So the next day, he loaded the donkey with bags of sponges. Sure enough, when the donkey went over the bridge, he jumped into the water and lay there, satisfied with his plan. But when he got to his hooves, his burden was harder to bear than usual. The sponges had soaked up the water, and the bags were as heavy as lead. He staggered wearily home under the load, wishing that he had been wiser. "I'll never again try to get out of working," he thought to himself. "Getting out of work is harder than just doing it in the first place."

Moral: Lazy people often end up working harder than anyone else!

Instructor: Why was the donkey unhappy?
Student: *The donkey was unhappy because the salt was so heavy.*

Instructor: What good things did the donkey get because of the salt?
Student: *He got grain and hay.*

Instructor: How did the donkey learn to get rid of the salt?
Student: *He fell into the water and the salt melted.*

Instructor: What did the donkey start doing on purpose?
Student: *He rolled in the water to melt the salt.*

Instructor: How did the merchant outsmart the donkey?
Student: *He filled the bags with sponges instead.*

Instructor: What happened when the donkey lay down in the water with the sponges?
Student: *The sponges soaked up water and got heavier and heavier.*

Instructor: Did that make life easier or harder for the donkey?
Student: *It made life harder.*

······· **LESSON 100** ·······

Parts of speech hunt

Note to Instructor: *Read through the following list of grammatical terms with the student. Then go back to the story "The Donkey and the Salt" in Lesson 99. As you read through the story together, ask the student to hunt for one of each of these grammatical terms. You might want to consider offering a small reward (such as raisins or chocolate chips) for each word that the student finds. Several answers are indicated in the Partial Key below; if necessary, you can drop hints. Encourage! This is a review, not a test.*

Grammatical Terms
noun
pronoun
adjective
action verb
linking verb
helping verb
adverb
preposition
article
conjunction
interjection
question
statement
exclamation
contraction
direct quotation
the pronoun "I" (capitalized)

Partial Key

article   noun   action verb   adjective   noun   preposition   pronoun

A   merchant who lived long ago often heaped   huge   bags of salt   upon   his   donkey's back

conjunction   preposition   article   noun   helping verb   action verb

and   drove the donkey   to   the market. There, he   would   sell the salt for a good price. He

linking verb   linking verb   adverb   adjective   conjunction

was   happy—but his donkey   was   discontent. The salt was tremendously heavy.   And

although the money that the merchant earned at the market bought the donkey good grain and

exclamation

sweet hay, the donkey complained about his work. "If only I didn't have to haul these bags of salt!"

statement or exclamation

he moaned. "My life would be so much easier!"

On his way to the market one day, the donkey stumbled on a little bridge over a stream and fell

statement   command

into the water. As he lay in the water, the salt melted and ran away down the stream. "Get up,"

the merchant ordered. When the donkey scrambled to his feet, the bags were empty. He felt

light and carefree! He switched his tail and trotted happily down the road, free of his burden.

The merchant was sad, for he made no money at the market. He returned home with empty

question   direct quotation   pronoun "I"

hands. "What will I do?" he asked himself. "Without my market days,   I   will no longer be able

to buy grain and hay for my donkey."

But the donkey was pleased with his day off. On his next trip to the market, he stumbled

again—this time on purpose! He rolled into the water and waited for the salt to melt. When the

interjection

bags were empty once more, he jumped to his feet and ambled cheerfully along. "Hurrah!"

contraction

he thought to himself. "I am free of my burden *again*! Now I know the secret. I   don't ever have

to carry salt to the market again."

The merchant realized that his lazy donkey had fallen on purpose. So the next day, he loaded

the donkey with bags of sponges. Sure enough, when the donkey went over the bridge, he jumped

into the water and lay there, satisfied with his plan. But when he got to his hooves, his burden was

harder to bear than usual. The sponges had soaked up the water, and the bags were as heavy as

contraction

lead. He staggered wearily home under the load, wishing that he had been wiser.   "I'll   never

again try to get out of working," he thought to himself. "Getting out of work is harder than just

doing it in the first place."

Glossary of Terms and Definitions

Terms

action verb—An action verb is a word that does an action.

adjective—An adjective is a word that describes a noun.

adverb—An adverb is a word that describes a verb, an adjective, or another adverb.

antonym—Antonyms are words that have opposite meanings.

article—The articles are "a," "an," and "the."

command—A command gives an order or makes a request.

common noun—A common noun is the name of any person, place, thing, or idea.

conjunction—A conjunction is a word that joins words or groups of words together.

contraction—A contraction is two words put together into one word with some letters left out.

direct quotation—A direct quotation is the exact words spoken by someone.

exclamation—An exclamation shows sudden or strong feeling.

helping verb—A helping verb is a verb that helps another verb.

indirect quotation—An indirect quotation tells what someone says but doesn't use their exact words.

interjection—An interjection is a word that expresses sudden or strong feeling.

linking verb—A linking verb is a word that links two words together.

noun—A noun is the name of a person, place, thing, or idea.

preposition—A preposition is a word that shows the relationship of a noun or pronoun to another word in the sentence.

pronoun—A pronoun is a word used in place of a noun.

proper noun—A proper noun is a word that names a particular person, place, thing, or idea.

question—A question asks something.

sentence—A sentence is a group of words that expresses a complete thought.

state of being verb—A state of being verb is a word that shows a state of being.

statement—A statement gives information.

synonym—Synonyms are words that have the same meaning.

verb—A verb is a word that does an action, shows a state of being, links two words together, or helps another verb.

Memorized Definitions of Parts of Speech

A noun is the name of a person, place, thing, or idea.

A pronoun is a word used in place of a noun.

A verb is a word that does an action, shows a state of being, links two words together, or helps another verb.

An adjective is a word that describes a noun.

An adverb is a word that describes a verb, an adjective, or another adverb.

A conjunction is a word that joins words or groups of words together.

An interjection is a word that expresses sudden or strong feeling.

A preposition is a word that shows the relationship of a noun or pronoun to another word in the sentence.

Capitalization and Punctuation Rules

Proper names begin with capital letters.

The pronoun "I" is always capitalized.

Capitalize the first word and every important word in the titles of poems, stories, and books.

Capitalize the beginning of every line in poetry.

Capitalize the names of the months, but not the names of the seasons.

Initials are capitalized and followed by periods.

Abbreviated titles of respect are capitalized and followed by periods.

An interjection all alone with an exclamation point should begin with a capital letter.

A sentence begins with a capital letter and ends with a punctuation mark.

A question ends with a question mark.

An exclamation ends with an exclamation point.

A statement ends with a period.

Put commas between items in a series.

In a date, a comma separates the day of the month and the year.

In an address, a comma separates the name of a city from the name of a state.

In a contraction, an apostrophe is put in the place of the missing letters.

The exact words a person says are always enclosed by quotation marks.

Memorized Lists

State of Being Verbs (and Linking Verbs)
am, is, are, was, were, be, being, been

Helping Verbs
am, is, are, was, were, be, being, been, have, has, had, do, does, did, shall, will, should, would, may, might, must, can, could

Articles
a, an, the

Conjunctions

and, but, or

Prepositions

aboard, about, above, across, after, against, along, among, around, at, before, behind, below, beneath, beside, between, beyond, by, down, during, except, for, from, in, inside, into, like, near, of, off, on, over, past, since, through, throughout, to, toward, under, underneath, until, up, upon, with, within, without

Poems

"The Goops"
Gelett Burgess ....pg 3
"The Year"
Sara Coleridge, adapted by Sara Buffington .... pg 68
"The Little Bird"
Mother Goose rhyme... pg 86
"The Months"
Mother Goose rhyme.. pg 117
"All Things Bright and Beautiful"
Cecil Alexander .... pg 207

Index

Action verbs (see Verbs)
Addresses
    capitalization, 37–39
    commas, 26–27
    on envelopes, 83, 166–167
    on postcards, 112–113
Adjectives
    definition, 235
    introduction, 51–52
    review, 122–123, 126–128, 189–191
Adverbs
    definition, 235
    introduction, 108–109
    review, 110–111, 122–123, 126–128, 153–154, 189–191
Alexander, Cecil, 207
Alice's Adventures in Wonderland, 106–107
"All Things Bright and Beautiful," 207
Antonyms,
    definition, 235
    introduction, 179–181
    review, 217–218
Apostrophes, 42, 43, 44, 63, 201, 214, 236
"April," 34–36
Articles
    definition, 235
    introduction, 129–131
    review, 132–134, 236
"At this the whole pack rose up into the air...," 106–107
Audubon, John James, 182
"August," 55–57

"Bed in Summer," 142–144
"Beneath the castle wall," 147–149
"Beneath the pyramids," 145–146
The Black Arrow, 40–41
"The brown bird," 73–74
"Brush your teeth," 179–181
Buffington, Sara, 22, 68, 116, 118, 124, 172
Burgess, Gelett, 3

"The Camel's Nose," 17–18
Capitalization
    addresses, 37–39
    "I," 7–8
    initials, 37–39

poems, 37–39
    proper names, 37–39
    review, 132–134
    rules, 236
    titles of respect, 37–39
Carroll, Lewis, 106
Coleridge, Sara, 22, 68, 116–117
Commands, 24, 70–71, 96–97, 235
    see also Sentences
Commas
    dates and addresses, 26–27
    in a series, 28–29
Conjunctions, 75–77, 235, 237
Contractions
    definition, 235
    introduction, 42–43
    review, 44–45, 63–64, 201–203
    using "not," 46–48
Copywork
    addressing postcards, 112–113
    "April," 36
    "August," 57
    "The baby and I," 7–8
    contractions, 42–45, 201–203
    days of the week, 116–118
    "December," 67
    "Emily Sang," 5–6
    "February," 26–27
    "The Goops," 3–4
    "January," 24–25
    "July," 53–54
    "June," 51–52
    "The Little Bird," 84–85
    "The Little Red Hen," 87–90
    "March," 30–33
    "May," 46–48
    "Not I," 91–92
    "November," 65–66
    "October," 63–64
    "Ouch!," 70–72
    purpose, xiii
    "September," 58–60
    "Snuggles, wiggles, grins, and giggles," 28–29
    state of being verbs, 9–10
    writing a letter, 164–165

writing postcards, 114–115
"The Year," 22–23
Cotman, Frederick George, 222
Cumulative review, 208–214
    Review session 1, 228
    Review session 2, 229
    Review session 3, 230

"The Daffodils," 149
Dates, 26–27
"Days of the Week," 118
Days of the week, 116–118
"December," 67
"Dick and Lawless in Holyrood Forest," 40–41
Dictation
    "Bed in Summer," 142–144
    "Beneath the castle wall," 147–149
    "Beneath the pyramids," 145–146
    "The brown bird," 73–74
    "Brush your teeth," 179–181
    "Dinosaurs," 119–121
    "The dump truck," 96–100
    "During my lesson," 150–152
    "God has made them so," 58–60
    "I ate my supper," 108–109
    "I was tired," 75–77
    "I'm coming to eat you up!," 104–105
    introduction, 49–50
    "King of the Stuffed Animals," 158–159
    "The Mother Cat," 198–200
    "Over my head," 135–137
    "Ow! Yuck! Oh!," 192–194
    "The Platypus," 186–188
    purpose, xiii
    review sessions, 228–230
    "Roller coasters," 176–178
    "Through the rain," 160–162
    "The troll," 217–219
    "What we did," 129–131
    "Who will help me?," 93–95
    "Whole Duty of Children," 110–111
    "Who's that trip-trapping?," 195–197
    "The zoo," 78–80
"Dinosaurs," 119–121
"The Donkey and the Salt," 231–234

"The dump truck," 96–100
"During my lesson," 150–152
Envelope, addressing, 83, 166–167
Exclamations, 25, 71, 97, 185, 236
    definition, 235
    see also Sentences

"February," 26–27
"Foreign Lands," 170

Glossary, 235–237
"God has made them so," 58–60
"The Goops," 3–4
Grammar, purpose of, xiv

Hokusai, Katsushika, 140
Homer, Winslow, 204
Homophones, 225–226
"How Creatures Move," 66

"I ate my supper," 108–109
"I Love You Well," 155–156
"I was tired," 75–77
"I'm coming to eat you up!," 104–105
Initials, 37–39
Interjections
    definition, 235
    introduction, 70–72
    review, 73, 75, 78, 135, 192

"January," 24–25
"July," 53–54
"June," 51–52

"King of the Stuffed Animals," 158–159

Language, teaching, xii
Lear, Edward, 208
Letter-writing
    addressing envelopes, 83, 166–167
    introduction, 164–165
    thank-you note, 81–82
    see also Postcards
Linking verbs (see Verbs)
"The Little Bird," 84–85, 86

"The Little Red Hen," 87–90

"March," 30–33, 49–50
"May," 46–48
Memorization
  "All Things Bright and Beautiful," 207
  "The Goops," 3–4
  lists, 224, 236–237
  "The Little Bird," 86
  purpose, xiii
  "The Year," 68–69
"The Months," 117–118
"The Mother Cat," 198–200
Mother Goose, 84, 86, 117–118, 155–156

Narration, picture
  "At this the whole pack rose up into the air...," 106–107
  "Dick and Lawless in Holyrood Forest," 40–41
  "The Great Wave off Kanagawa," 140–141
  "One of the Family," 222–223
  purpose, xiii–xiv
  "Snap the Whip," 204–205
  "Snowy owls," 182–183
Narration, story
  "The Camel's Nose," 17–19
  "The Donkey and the Salt," 231–234
  "The Little Red Hen," 87–90
  purpose, xiii–xiv
  "The Quarrel," 61–62
  "The Storm," 124–128
  "The Three Bears," 172–175
  "The Three Billy Goats Gruff," 101–103
"Not I," 91–92
Nouns
  common, 235
  definition, 235
  described by adjectives, 51–52
  introduction, 1–2
  proper, 37, 235
  relationship to prepositions, 135–136, 138, 142, 145, 147, 153, 158–159, 166, 215
  review, 34–36, 55, 71, 75, 114, 198, 209, 220–221
"November," 65–66

"October," 63–64

"The Old Man and His Nose," 208
"One of the Family," 222–223
"Ouch!," 70–72
"Over my head," 135–137
"Ow! Yuck! Oh!," 192–194

Parts of speech
  definitions, 235–236
  hunt, 233–234
  introduction, 75–77
  review, 220–221
Periods, 37,38, 39, 50, 60, 70, 72, 81, 83, 93, 96, 97, 104, 111, 112, 134, 144, 165, 166, 185, 213, 236
"The Platypus," 186–188
Poems
  "All Things Bright and Beautiful," 207
  "Bed in Summer," 144
  capitalization, 37–39
  cumulative review, 163, 227
  "The Daffodils," 149
  "Days of the Week," 118
  "Foreign Lands," 170
  "The Goops," 3–4
  "How Creatures Move," 66
  "I Love You Well," 155–156
  "The Little Bird," 84, 86
  memorization, 68–69, 238
  "The Months," 117–118
  "The Old Man and His Nose," 208
  "The Tutor," 225–226
  "Whole Duty of Children," 111
  "The Wind," 33
  "The Year," 22–23, 116–117
Poetry, booklet, 22–23
Postcards
  addressing, 112–113
  writing, 114–115
  see also Letter-writing
Prepositions
  and adverbs, 153–154
  definition, 235
  introduction, 135–137
  and letter-writing, 164–165
  review, 155–157, 168–171, 215–216, 237
  showing relationships, 138–139, 142–152, 158–162

Pronouns, 5–6, 235
Proper names, 37–39
Punctuation
    apostrophes, 42–43
    commas, 26–29
    quotation marks, 84–85
    rules, 236
    see also commas; periods, question marks; quotation
    marks

"The Quarrel," 61–62
Questions, 24–25, 71, 97, 235
    see also Sentences
Question Marks, 71, 97, 185, 211, 236
Quotation marks, 84–85
Quotations
    direct, 84–85, 235
    indirect, 91–92, 235

Rackham, Arthur, 106
"Roller coasters," 176–178

Seasons, 24–25
Sentences
    definition, 235
    types of, 24–25, 185
"September," 58–60
"Snap the Whip," 204–205
"Snuggles, wiggles, grins and giggles," 28–29
State of being (see Verbs)
Statements, 24, 70, 96, 235
    see also Sentences
Stevenson, Robert Louis, 33, 111, 144, 170
"The Storm," 124–128
Synonyms, 176–178, 235

Thank-you note, 81–82
"The Three Bears," 172–175
"The Three Billy Goats Gruff," 101–103
"Through the rain," 160–162
Titles (of respect), 37–39
"The troll," 217–219
"The Tutor," 225–226

Verbs
    action verbs, 7–8, 235
    definition, 235
    helping verbs, 30–33, 235, 236
Verbs (*continued*)
    linking verbs, 13–16, 20–21, 235–236
    review, 155–157
    state of being, 9–12, 235–236

Wells, Carolyn, 225
"What we did," 129–131
"Who will help me?," 93–95
"Whole Duty of Children," 110–111
"Who's that trip-trapping?," 195–197
"The Wind," 33
Wordsworth, William, 149

"The Year," 22–23, 68–69, 116–117